CHÂTEAUX
OF THE
LOIRE VALLEY

Châteaux of the Loire Valley

Text
Jean-Marie Pérouse de Montclos
Photographs
Robert Polidori

KÖNEMANN

Translation: Paul Aston for Hart McLeod, Cambridge
Editing: Rosalind Horton, Chris Miller
Typesetting: Goodfellow & Egan Publishing Management, Cambridge
Production manager: Detlev Schaper
Printing and binding: Mladinska knijga tiskarna d. d., Ljubljana

Printed in Slovenia

ISBN 3-89508-598-7

10 9 8 7 6 5 4 3 2 1

CONTENTS

Laval

M a i n e

Le Mans

Verdelles

Château-
Gontier

Saint-Ouen

Mortier-Crolles

Marche de

La Flèche

Châteaubriant

Segré

Le Lude

Bretagne

Le Plessis-Macé

Le Plessis-Bourré

A n j o u

Baugé

Angers

Montgeoffroy

Loire

Serrant

Ancenis

Luynes

Brissac

Langeais

Boumois

Villan...

Nantes

Goulaine

Saumur

Les Réaux

Ussé

Montsoreau

Azay-le-
Rideau

Lac de
Grand-Lieu

Chinon

T o...

Montreuil-Bellay

Cholet

Champigny-
sur-Veude

Argenton

Oiron

Châtellerault

Bressuire

V
e
n
d
La Roche-sur-Yon

é

Parthenay

P o i t o u

Les Sables-d'Olonne

e

Poitiers

Fontenay-le-Comte

A t l a n t i c

A u n i s

Niort

O c e a n

La Rochelle

987	Election of Hugh Capet.
987–1040	Foulques Nerra, Count of Anjou.
1023	Establishment of the County of Blois-Champagne.
1066	William of Normandy (the Conqueror) becomes King of England.
1095	Preaching of the First Crusade.
1118	Foundation of the Order of Templars.
1122	Abbot Suger installed at St Denis.
1129	Matilda of England (the Empress Maud) marries Geoffrey Plantagenet, Count of Anjou.
1137	Eleanor of Aquitaine marries Louis VII.
1152	Louis VII repudiates Eleanor, who immediately marries Henry Plantagenet.
1163	Work begins on cathedral of Notre-Dame de Paris.
1179	Philippe Auguste crowned.
1187–88	Philippe Auguste captures Berry and enters Touraine.
1197–99	Philippe wars with Richard the Lionheart, King of England.
1199	John Lackland succeeds Richard the Lionheart.
1205	Philippe Auguste conquers Touraine and Anjou.
1214	French victory at Bouvines against Flemish, English and Holy Roman Emperor Otto.
1245	Construction of the Sainte Chapelle in Paris.
1248	St. Louis (Louis IX) joins the Crusade.
1270	Louis IX dies in Tunis.
1307	Philippe IV suppresses Templar order in France.
1328	Advent of Philippe VI of Valois. Edward III of England claims French crown. [1337]
1356	Edward's son the Black Prince captures King Jean le Bon at the Battle of Poitiers. The Dauphin Charles becomes regent.
1358	Provost Stephen Marcel raises Paris against the Dauphin.
1364	Jean le Bon dies in London, having returned voluntarily as hostage. Dauphin becomes Charles V.
1368	War resumes between French and English.
1370	Bertrand du Guesclin becomes Constable of France.
1380	Death of Charles V.
1392	Madness of Charles VI.
1408–1416	*Très Riches Heures* du duc de Berry (book of hours) created.
1414	Henry V, King of England, claims Plantagenet legacy in France.
1415	Henry V defeats French at Azincourt.
1422	Henry V dies at castle of Vincennes. Charles VI dies insane.
1429	Joan of Arc meets the Dauphin Charles at Chinon. Charles crowned.

1431	Joan of Arc burnt at the stake in Rouen.
1436	Charles VII enters Paris.
1450	English defeated at Formigny.
1453	Treaty of Arras ends Hundred Years' War.
1480	René of Anjou dies as Count of Provence and King of Jerusalem.
1484	Anjou reclaimed as royal possession.
1489–1490	First six books of Philippe de Commynes's Memoirs.
1491	The French occupy Brittany, Anne de Bretagne marries Charles VIII.
1495	Charles VIII enters Naples wearing the Imperial robe and the quadruple crown of France, Naples, Jerusalem and Constantinople – and lasts three months.
1512	French driven out of Italy.
1515	François I reconquers Milan at battle of Marignano by defeating Swiss.
1515–1524	Construction of François I wing at Blois.
1519	Construction of Chambord and death of Leonardo da Vinci at Clos-Lucé.
1524	French hero Captain Bayard dies in Piedmont.
1525	François I taken prisoner at battle of Pavia.
1527	Troops of Holy Roman Emperor Charles V sack Rome.
1532	Rabelais's *Pantagruel* appears.
1534	Rabelais's *Gargantua* appears.
1544	Death of poet Clément Marot.
1546	Reconstruction of the Louvre begins.
1549	Joachim du Bellay († 1560), friend of poet Pierre Ronsard († 1580), writes *Défense de la langue française*, a plea for return to classical models.
1562	Massacre of Protestants at Vassy.
1562–1598	Wars of Religion.
1572	Massacre of St. Bartholomew.
1580	Montaigne's *Essays* appear.
1588	Henri III has Catholic League leader Duc Henri de Guise assassinated.
1589	Catherine de' Medici dies. Henri III murdered.
1593	Henri IV crowned at Chartres after renouncing Protestantism.
1598	Edict of Nantes secures rights for Protestants.
1600	Henri marries Maria de' Medici.
1610	Henri IV assassinated.
1635	French Academy founded.
1636	Corneille's play *Le Cid* appears.
1637	Descartes publishes his *Discours*.
1642	Cardinal Richelieu dies.
1643	Regency of Anne of Austria follows death of Louis XIII. Spaniards forced to abandon siege of Rocroi.

1648	Treaty of Westphalia ends Thirty Years' War.
1659	Peace of the Pyrenees ends war with Spain.
1661	Louis XIV commences direct government.
1662	Blaise Pascal dies.
1664	Colbert becomes Superintendent of Works.
1666	Molière's *Misanthrope*.
1671	Academy of Architecture founded.
1673	Molière dies.
1677	Racine's *Phèdre*.
1683	Colbert dies.
1684	Playwright Pierre Corneille dies.
1685	Edict of Nantes revoked.
1690	Death of painter Le Brun.
1699	Death of playwright Racine.
1700	Death of landscape gardener Le Nôtre
1702–1704	Calvinist Camisards revolt.
1708	Death of Louis XIV's architect Hardouin-Mansart.
1715	Death of Louis XIV.
1734	Montesquieu's *Considérations*.
1742	Jacques-Ange Gabriel becomes royal architect.
1745	Madame de Pompadour becomes royal favorite.
1751	First volume of Diderot & Alembert's Encyclopedia.
1761	Rousseau's *Nouvelle Héloise*.
1762–68	Gabriel builds the Petit Trianon.
1766	Louis XV acquires Lorraine.
1770	Death of painter Boucher.
1774	Death of Louis XV.
1777	La Fayette takes part in American War of Independence.
1778	Death of Voltaire and Jean-Jacques Rousseau.
1789	Opening of States General, fall of the Bastille.
1793	Execution of Louis XVI.
1799	Napoleon's coup of 18th Brumaire.
1804	Napoleon crowned Emperor.
1805	Victory over Austrians and Russians at Austerlitz.
1814	Napoleon abdicates.
1815	Napoleon defeated at Waterloo.
1825	Death of painter Louis David.
1848	Louis Philippe abdicates, republic proclaimed.
1852	Louis Napoleon becomes Emperor Napoleon III.

GENEALOGY OF THE KINGS OF FRANCE

I. MEROVINGIANS

Clovis
(reigned 481–511)

II. CAROLINGIANS

Charlemagne
(reigned 771–814)

III. ROBERTIANS

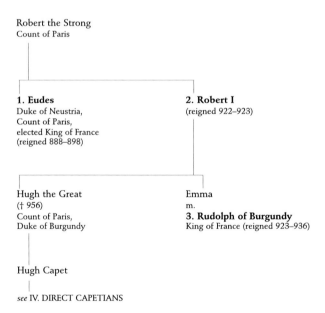

Robert the Strong
Count of Paris

1. Eudes
Duke of Neustria,
Count of Paris,
elected King of France
(reigned 888–898)

2. Robert I
(reigned 922–923)

Hugh the Great
(† 956)
Count of Paris,
Duke of Burgundy

Emma
m.
3. Rudolph of Burgundy
King of France (reigned 923–936)

Hugh Capet

see IV. DIRECT CAPETIANS

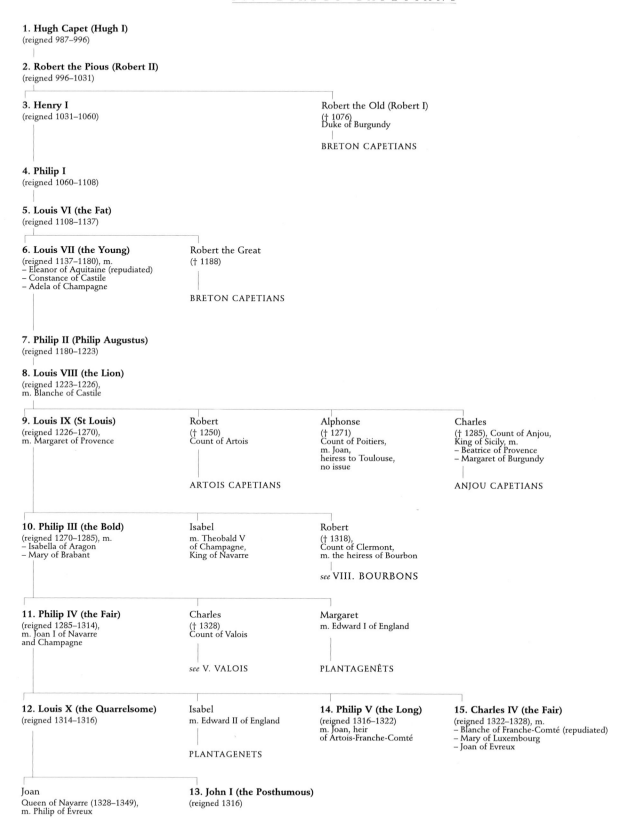

1. Hugh Capet (Hugh I)
(reigned 987–996)

2. Robert the Pious (Robert II)
(reigned 996–1031)

3. Henry I
(reigned 1031–1060)

Robert the Old (Robert I)
(† 1076)
Duke of Burgundy

BRETON CAPETIANS

4. Philip I
(reigned 1060–1108)

5. Louis VI (the Fat)
(reigned 1108–1137)

6. Louis VII (the Young)
(reigned 1137–1180), m.
– Eleanor of Aquitaine (repudiated)
– Constance of Castile
– Adela of Champagne

Robert the Great
(† 1188)

BRETON CAPETIANS

7. Philip II (Philip Augustus)
(reigned 1180–1223)

8. Louis VIII (the Lion)
(reigned 1223–1226),
m. Blanche of Castile

9. Louis IX (St Louis)
(reigned 1226–1270),
m. Margaret of Provence

Robert
(† 1250)
Count of Artois

ARTOIS CAPETIANS

Alphonse
(† 1271)
Count of Poitiers,
m. Joan,
heiress to Toulouse,
no issue

Charles
(† 1285), Count of Anjou,
King of Sicily, m.
– Beatrice of Provence
– Margaret of Burgundy

ANJOU CAPETIANS

10. Philip III (the Bold)
(reigned 1270–1285), m.
– Isabella of Aragon
– Mary of Brabant

Isabel
m. Theobald V
of Champagne,
King of Navarre

Robert
(† 1318),
Count of Clermont,
m. the heiress of Bourbon

see VIII. BOURBONS

11. Philip IV (the Fair)
(reigned 1285–1314),
m. Joan I of Navarre
and Champagne

Charles
(† 1328)
Count of Valois

see V. VALOIS

Margaret
m. Edward I of England

PLANTAGENÊTS

12. Louis X (the Quarrelsome)
(reigned 1314–1316)

Isabel
m. Edward II of England

PLANTAGENETS

14. Philip V (the Long)
(reigned 1316–1322)
m. Joan, heir
of Artois-Franche-Comté

15. Charles IV (the Fair)
(reigned 1322–1328), m.
– Blanche of Franche-Comté (repudiated)
– Mary of Luxembourg
– Joan of Evreux

Joan
Queen of Navarre (1328–1349),
m. Philip of Évreux

13. John I (the Posthumous)
(reigned 1316)

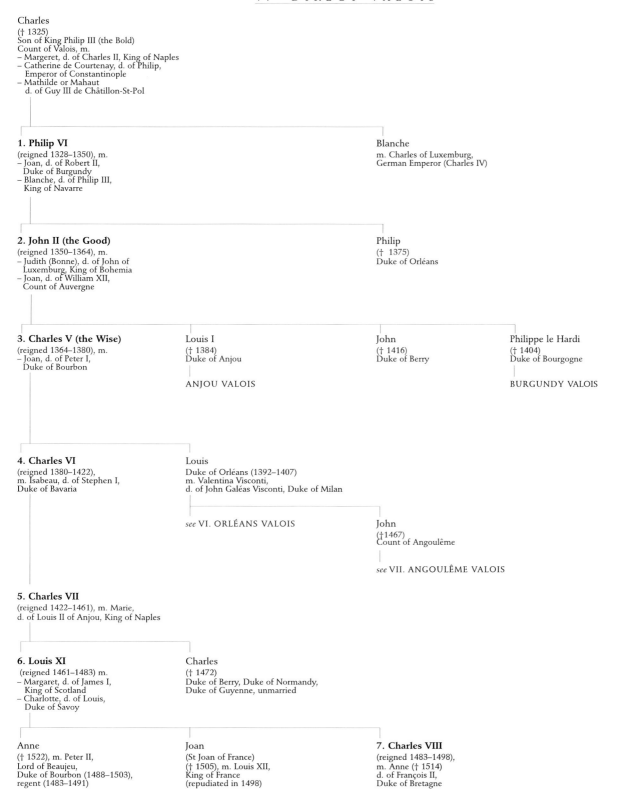

Charles
(† 1325)
Son of King Philip III (the Bold)
Count of Valois, m.
– Margeret, d. of Charles II, King of Naples
– Catherine de Courtenay, d. of Philip,
  Emperor of Constantinople
– Mathilde or Mahaut
  d. of Guy III de Châtillon-St-Pol

1. Philip VI
(reigned 1328–1350), m.
– Joan, d. of Robert II,
  Duke of Burgundy
– Blanche, d. of Philip III,
  King of Navarre

Blanche
m. Charles of Luxemburg,
German Emperor (Charles IV)

2. John II (the Good)
(reigned 1350–1364), m.
– Judith (Bonne), d. of John of
  Luxemburg, King of Bohemia
– Joan, d. of William XII,
  Count of Auvergne

Philip
(† 1375)
Duke of Orléans

3. Charles V (the Wise)
(reigned 1364–1380), m.
– Joan, d. of Peter I,
  Duke of Bourbon

Louis I
(† 1384)
Duke of Anjou

ANJOU VALOIS

John
(† 1416)
Duke of Berry

Philippe le Hardi
(† 1404)
Duke of Bourgogne

BURGUNDY VALOIS

4. Charles VI
(reigned 1380–1422),
m. Isabeau, d. of Stephen I,
Duke of Bavaria

Louis
Duke of Orléans (1392–1407)
m. Valentina Visconti,
d. of John Galéas Visconti, Duke of Milan

see VI. ORLÉANS VALOIS

John
(†1467)
Count of Angoulême

see VII. ANGOULÊME VALOIS

5. Charles VII
(reigned 1422–1461), m. Marie,
d. of Louis II of Anjou, King of Naples

6. Louis XI
 (reigned 1461–1483) m.
– Margaret, d. of James I,
  King of Scotland
– Charlotte, d. of Louis,
  Duke of Savoy

Charles
(† 1472)
Duke of Berry, Duke of Normandy,
Duke of Guyenne, unmarried

Anne
(† 1522), m. Peter II,
Lord of Beaujeu,
Duke of Bourbon (1488–1503),
regent (1483–1491)

Joan
(St Joan of France)
(† 1505), m. Louis XII,
King of France
(repudiated in 1498)

7. Charles VIII
(reigned 1483–1498),
m. Anne († 1514)
d. of François II,
Duke of Bretagne

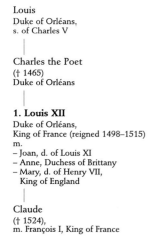

Louis
Duke of Orléans,
s. of Charles V

Charles the Poet
(† 1465)
Duke of Orléans

1. Louis XII
Duke of Orléans,
King of France (reigned 1498–1515)
m.
– Joan, d. of Louis XI
– Anne, Duchess of Brittany
– Mary, d. of Henry VII,
   King of England

Claude
(† 1524),
m. François I, King of France

V I I .   A N G O U L Ê M E   V A L O I S

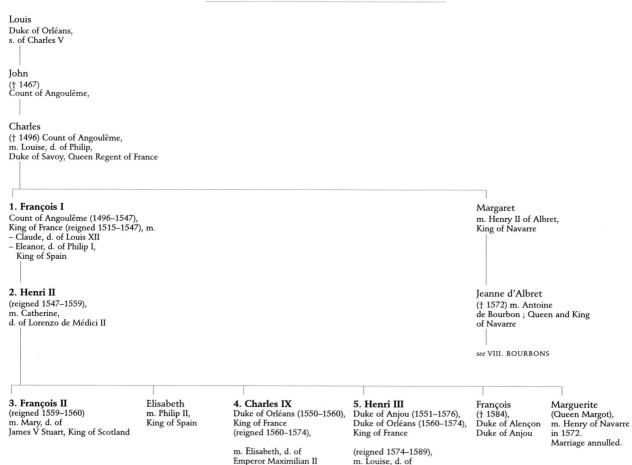

Louis
Duke of Orléans,
s. of Charles V

John
(† 1467)
Count of Angoulême,

Charles
(† 1496) Count of Angoulême,
m. Louise, d. of Philip,
Duke of Savoy, Queen Regent of France

1. François I
Count of Angoulême (1496–1547),
King of France (reigned 1515–1547), m.
– Claude, d. of Louis XII
– Eleanor, d. of Philip I,
   King of Spain

Margaret
m. Henry II of Albret,
King of Navarre

2. Henri II
(reigned 1547–1559),
m. Catherine,
d. of Lorenzo de Médici II

Jeanne d'Albret
(† 1572) m. Antoine
de Bourbon ; Queen and King
of Navarre

see VIII. BOURBONS

3. François II
(reigned 1559–1560)
m. Mary, d. of
James V Stuart, King of Scotland

Elisabeth
m. Philip II,
King of Spain

4. Charles IX
Duke of Orléans (1550–1560),
King of France
(reigned 1560–1574),

m. Élisabeth, d. of
Emperor Maximilian II

5. Henri III
Duke of Anjou (1551–1576),
Duke of Orléans (1560–1574),
King of France

(reigned 1574–1589),
m. Louise, d. of
Nicolas, Duke of Lorraine

François
(† 1584),
Duke of Alençon
Duke of Anjou

Marguerite
(Queen Margot),
m. Henry of Navarre
in 1572.
Marriage annulled.

1. Henri IV
s. of Antoine de Bourbon et Jeanne d'Albret,
King and Queen of Navarre.
King of Navarre (as Henri III),
Duke of Bourbon (1562–1589),
King of France and Navarre
(reigned 1589–1610), m.
– Marguerite of Valois,
   Queen Margot, d. of Henri II
– Maria de Medici (in 1600)

2. Louis XIII	Elisabeth	Marie-Christine	Gaston	Henriette
King of France and Navarre,	m. Philip IV of Spain	m. Victor Amadeus I	(† 1660)	m. Charles I
m. Anne of Austria		de Savoy	Duke of Orléans, m.	King of England
(reigned 1610–1643)			– Marie de Bourbon-Montpensier	
			– Marguerite of Lorraine	

3. Louis XIV
King of France and Navarre
(reigned 1643–1715), m.
Maria-Theresia of Austria

Philippe
(† 1701) Duke of Orléans, m.
– Henrietta of England
– Charlotte, Princess Palatine

see IX. ORLÉANS

Louis
(† 1711),
Grand Dauphin, m.
Marie Anna Christine of Bavaria

Louis	Philippe	Charles
(† 1712)	(† 1746)	(† 1714)
Duke of Bourgogne,	Duke of Anjou, King of Spain	Duke of Berry
dauphin,		
m. Marie-Adélaïde of Savoy		

SPANISH BOURBONS

4. Louis XV
Duke of Anjou, then dauphin
(1712–1715), King of France and
Navarre (reigned 1715–1774),
m. Maria Leszczynska

Louis
(† 1765)
dauphin, m.
– Maria Theresia of Spain
– Maria Josepha of Saxony

5. Louis XVI	**7. Louis XVIII**	**8. Charles X**
initially Louis Auguste,	Count of Provence,	(† en 1836)
Duke of Berry, then dauphin (1765–1774),	"King" 1795–1824,	Count of Artois,
King of France and Navarre (1774–1791),	effectively 1814–1815	King of France (1824–1830)
King of the French (1791–1792),	and 1815–1824,	m. Maria Theresia
m. Maria Antonietta of Austria	m. Louisa Maria	of Sardinia-Savoy
	of Sardinia-Savoy	

6. Louis « XVII »
dauphin (1789–1793)
then "King" (1793–1795)

Louis-Antoine	Charles-Ferdinand
(† 1844)	(† 1820), Duke of Berry
Duke of Angoulême	m. Maria Caroline
	of Bourbon-Sicily

Henri V
(† 1883),
Duke of Bordeaux,
Count of Chambord

I X .   O R L É A N S

1. Louis-Philippe
(† 1850)
descendant of Louis XIII,
Duke of Orléans (1793–1830),
King of the French (1830–1848)

INTRODUCTION

Typical scenery of the central part of the Loire Valley, seen from the gardens of the château of Menars.

How inclusive is the category "châteaux of the Loire"? At Ligeret, the source of the Loire (Latin name *liger*) stands a little château with as good a claim as any. It is normally excluded in favour of châteaux sited on tributaries, near confluences or simply on the banks of rivers whose waters eventually reach the Loire.

Geography and history intersect in a region where numerous celebrated châteaux are found: the Loire Valley. Here the river is wide and shallow except when in spate; then the banks themselves are at risk. Who has not heard the litany of the Loire Valley: the resort of kings, the garden of France, the land of arts and letters, and the cradle of the Renaissance.

But however far any Ligerian château may lie from this celebrated region, it must at least be on one of the routes that lead there; it

must be on one of the itineraries that tourist offices show converging there or be included in one of the quadrants into which cartographers divide the valley.

Should we include châteaux influenced by a style which bore the royal *imprimatur* and spread throughout the kingdom? On the banks of the Lignon, celebrated in the pastoral narratives of Honoré d'Urfé's l'*Astrée*, stands the château of La Bastie d'Urfé, a Renaissance masterpiece but one that has never been included among the châteaux of the Loire. True, the dainty Lignon joins the Loire above Roanne, as a torrential stream that defies navigation.

If we had to define the course of the Loire by just three points, we should probably take Roanne, Orléans and the confluence

with the Maine, near Angers. It is no accident that these three points are also important in the history of the river. At Roanne, the Loire is already 125 miles from its source, and has 500 navigable miles to run. From here, the Saône is only 60 or so miles away as the crow flies. Thus Charles VIII, setting off on the first Italian expedition, was forced to make a single transhipment between Amboise and Naples, his goal.

In prehistory, the Loire flowed into the Seine. It has retained an arc-shaped reminder of this, of which Orléans is the mid-point and northernmost extremity. The royal demesne,

The series of valleys united by the Loire Valley are characteristic of the mid-course of the river only.

It is as if history itself were governed by the Loire; as if the fortunes of the royal demesne were determined by its high and low waters. The normal "course" of its history was steady growth, but its waters often "fell" less as a result of retrenchment after wars had been lost than of the curious and deplorable practice of *apanage. Apanages* are parts of the demesne that the sovereign gave to his brothers or younger sons and which reverted to the crown when these male lines died out.

Under the 10th-century Frankish king Hugh Capet, the province of Orléans formed part of the kingdom. The rivalry between Orléans and Paris for the status of capital city ended in the 13th century in victory for Paris. It was a lasting victory, though events occasionally forced the kings to transfer their principal seats to the Loire Valley. In 1344, the Duchy of Orléans was created, an *apanage* that would not revert to the crown until the Duke himself became King of France under the name of Louis XII (1498). The title of Duke of Orléans was still given to the brothers of Louis XIII and Louis XIV and preserved by their descendants. Although a purely honorary title, it nonetheless long served as a cloak for intrigue and conspiracy, as witness Philippe-Égalité, Duke of Orléans and regicide during the Revolution, and his son Louis-Philippe I.

The county of Blois, which during the early years of the Capetian dynasty belonged to one of the most powerful lords in the king-

The castle of Angers was constructed by Louis IX while still a minor. Angers was at the time the western limit of Capetian territory, on the side facing the military threat from the Duke of Brittany and the King of England.

i.e. the territory which, in the Middle Ages, was ruled directly by the king, reunited the two rivers between Paris and Orléans. It was a union which produced a powerful dynasty, imposing its feudal rule on the dukes and barons of the kingdom. It was another union in 1491, at the onset of the Renaissance, that put an end to the ideas of independence harbored by one of the last duchies, when Anne de Bretagne, heir to Brittany, married King Charles VIII. The lands of the Duchy of Brittany, whose capital at Nantes lies on the Loire, began downstream of the confluence with the Maine. The shared channel of the Maine carries the waters of the Sarthe and Loir rivers as well, and as a result the lower Loire is still navigable today. Constricted by the gorges of the Massif Central where it rises, the Loire is again intermittently confined when it reaches the Massif Armoricain.

The room at Blois known as the States Room. This exceptionally large room hosted assemblies of the States General in 1576 and 1588.

dom, was bought in 1391 by the Duke of Orléans, and so took the borders of his duchy downstream again. Still further downstream, the county and later duchy of Touraine became part of the royal demesne in the mid-13th century, its fate matching that of the Duchy of Orléans. The *apanage* reverted to the king from time to time, but the title lost nothing of its nuisance value.

Destiny had the same fate in store – but on a broader historical canvas – for Anjou, which later extended as far as the banks of the river. When Hugh Capet came to the throne, his powerful vassal Foulques Nerra,

The keep and chapel of the castle of Châteaudun.

took over the title of Count. The valley echoed with blows exchanged by the Counts of Anjou and Blois. The first House of Anjou, Foulques and Plantagenet, provided kings for London and Jerusalem. The English king Henry II, who was Count of Anjou and Duke of Normandy, married Eleanor, who brought him Aquitaine. The confrontation between the kings of France and England was to last until the middle of the 15th century. Philippe Auguste incorporated Anjou into the royal demesne in 1205. In 1246, the title of Anjou was given to Charles, brother of Louis IX, who became King of Sicily. His descendants would carry the Angevin name as far afield as Hungary and Poland. However, in 1289 Anjou was ceded to the Valois, who restored it to the Crown when they seized the latter. In 1360, Anjou was made a duchy for the benefit of Louis, son of Jean II le Bon. It finally reverted to the royal demesne in 1481, as part of the inheritance of René, the famous René le Bon, nominal King of Sicily. The title of Duke of Anjou remained a peregrine one, with both Henry, King of Poland before he became Henri III of France, and Philip V, King of Spain and grandson of Louis XIV, bearing it. We might almost classify the Castel Nuovo in Naples, built by the Angevins in the late 13th century, among the châteaux of the Loire!

It would be closer to the truth to define the Loire Valley as coincidental with the duchies of Orléans, Touraine and Anjou. In the west, the frontier remained distinct right up to the Revolution, since Brittany preserved its own identity with the status of a *pays*. But we cannot exclude Berry, which is traversed by quite a number of left-bank tributaries and was, under its Duke Jean, a heartland of that pre-Renaissance whose influence pervaded the châteaux of the High Renaissance. The duchy was created in 1360 for the son of Jean II le Bon, who was also called Jean. He died without issue, and in 1434, Berry reverted to the Crown, just in time to provide the Valois with a refuge and a capital in the struggle against the English. Charles VII was nicknamed the King of Bourges.

With Nevers situated on the Loire and Moulins on the Allier (the main tributary on the left bank), the Nivernais and the Bourbonnais – both upstream of Berry – also have some title to inclusion in the Ligerian union. The château of Nevers is described by some guides as an "authentic château of the Loire." The same could be said of Moulins, where Anne de France, better known under the name Anne de Beaujeu, wife of Pierre de Beaujeu, the Duke of Bourbon, regent during the minority of Charles VIII and during the expedition to Naples, garnered the first fruits of the Italian Renaissance.

The Renaissance is only one phase in the artistic history of the Loire. The easily defended sites, natural mounds surrounded by water and plateaus dominating valleys, have been occupied since time immemorial. A distinction is still made between châteaux which are quaintly termed aquatic in contrast to the *châteaux d'éperon* (castles built on spurs or salients). The technique of the *éperon barré* (barred spur) consists of fortifying a narrow promontory by means of a moat. The confluences of the Loire Valley produce terrain

The castle of Langeais, constructed by Louis XI in the austere style he preferred.

particularly well-suited to this, as most of the tributaries follow a course almost parallel to the Loire before joining up with it. The moats are quite remarkable achievements, sunken works of architecture, whose excavation often supplied material for the superstructures. However, the châteaux appear not to have been built of stone before the 10th century. It seems likely that stone buildings first appeared with the advent of the Capetians (987). Among the first stone-built

châteaux to be mentioned are those constructed by Thibaud le Tricheur, Count of Blois, at Blois, Chinon and Châteaudun. Châteaudun is the capital of the Dunois region, which belonged to the Counts of Blois. It is situated on the Loir, which runs virtually parallel to the Loire; there are thus many reasons for including this northern château in the Ligerian family.

The oldest keeps extant today are at Langeais and Loches, both attributed to

The great hall of the château of Amboise.

Foulques Nerra, Count of Anjou (late 10th–early 11th century). The keep at Loches is exemplary in several respects. This huge square tower stands directly above the deep moat barring the spur. The entrance, high up on its side, is served by a second, smaller rectangular tower. Nothing remains of Foulques Nerra's works at Amboise,

Door of the staircase at the castle of Verdelles, a good example of the Flamboyant Gothic style.

OPPOSITE:
Jean, Duke of Berry, at table in the Très Riches Heures du duc de Berry, *in the month of January. Early 15th century, Musée Condé, Chantilly. It was at the Duke of Berry's castles, notably that of Mehun-sur-Yèvre, that the Flamboyant style was born.*

slightly earlier. Also at Blois, the county seat, the most remarkable feudal room has been preserved, dating from the beginning of the 13th century. A few decades later, during the minority of Louis IX, the royal castles of Saumur and Angers were built, guarding on left and right banks Anjou land conquered by Philippe Auguste. At Saumur, later transformations have overlaid what was a fortress conceived entirely for defensive rather than residential purposes. At Angers it is still possible to identify the original layout of the fortress.

There seems to be little of note in the history of the Ligerian castle between the construction of the fortress at Angers around 1230 and the creation of the Duchies of Anjou and Berry in 1360. A pacified province and triumphant capital made of the 13th the century of St. Louis (Louis IX). The French Gothic style known as Rayonnant sprang up at the royal Abbey of Saint-Denis, also around 1230. The only examples of it in the Loire Valley are churches. The advent of the Valois (1328), the supreme Ligerian dynasty, had no immediate effect, if we except some disastrous battles in the Hundred Years' War. War did not encourage construction. In contrast, the creation of the duchies of Anjou and Berry by Jean II le Bon in 1360 made these *apanages*, which carried the prestige of States General, into focal points for the later Flamboyant Gothic, an early Renaissance style that was purely French. The style received further stimulus when peace returned during the reign of Charles V (1364–1380). The architectural works of the King were

Montrésor and Montbazon, but the lower parts of the keep at Beaugency probably date from the same period as the keep at Loches.

The main development in the history of the keep was the change from the rectangular or square plan to the circular plan. This innovation did not originate with Philippe Auguste's engineers, but it was certainly they who popularized the formula. The Coudray Tower at the château of Chinon is one of these Augustan keeps (1205) while the Count of Blois's keep at Châteaudun is perhaps

Castle of Saumur, built by Louis, Duke of Anjou, brother of Charles V and Jean, Duke of Berry. This castle is a good example of the pre-Renaissance style of the second half of the 14th century. In the foreground is a bastion from the late 16th century.

concentrated on the Île de France, effectively meaning Paris, but the work of his ducal brothers was Ligerian. The *Très Riches Heures*, brilliantly illuminated for the Duke of Berry, preserve the memory of these châteaux.

The most remarkable château, Mehun-sur-Yèvre, is sadly now no more than a ruin. The improvements ordered by Jean de Berry to make an ancient castle habitable have completely disappeared. The entrance façade – though particularly vulnerable – was entirely in pierced work. The towers were topped with curious openwork belvederes. This technique for lightening walls is now only represented in the Loire Valley by

churches (Bourges, Tours), the Duke of Anjou's château of Saumur, Châteaudun, and in the house at Bourges that Jacques Cœur built for himself. Cœur, the royal treasurer, was the most illustrious example of the rising bourgeoisie. By virtue of services rendered to the throne, the bourgeoise came to fill all the positions that had previously been reserved for the great feudal lords.

France had just endured the grimmest decades of the Hundred Years' War. Charles VII had been forced to abandon Bourges, which was too close to hostile Burgundy, and escape to Chinon, where good fortune arrived at last in the shape of Joan of Arc. Jacques Cœur, who financed the reconquest of the kingdom, thought that the good times of the dukes had returned. An unlucky notion, as it turned out. His trial and the confiscation of his goods ushered in a period of relatively architectural austerity, as if all energy had to be devoted to economic and political reconstruction. The austere reign of Louis XI (1461–1483) dominated the second half of the century. The most important Ligerian château of Louis XI is Langeais. It is hard to believe that it was not built at the height of the war, so ravaged is it. The little château of Plessis-lès-Tours seems to have been more attractive, although we must use our imagination to supply the iron bars, moineaux, and pins Louis XI used to defend it; they prompted the contemporary chronicler Philippe de Commynes to compare it to the iron cages in which Louis incarcerated his prisoners.

Once disarmed, Plessis-lès-Tours exemplified the vogue for *manoirs*. The fashion was

started by René le Bon, who in his homeland of Anjou abandoned the great fortified castles for undefended country houses that are almost bourgeois, if that term could ever be applied to the nominal King of Sicily. Yet the term applies equally to his cousin the King of France. How Louis XI surrounded himself with new men of humble origins is a familiar story. Among them was Jean Bourré. Applying decoration sparingly so as not to irritate the thrifty monarch, Bourré showed at Plessis-Bourré how the medieval castle could be opened up to admit air and light. The same approach can be seen at the

Château of Chambord, built by François I. It is a perfect example of a Renaissance royal château in the Loire Valley.

Château of Chenonceaux astride the River Cher. In the foreground is the château constructed by Thomas Bohier in the early 16th century on the foundations of a mill. In the background is the bridge with the double row of galleries built by Diane de Poitiers and Catherine de'Medici in the second half of the 16th century.

château of Gien, built for Anne de Beaujeu. It is constructed almost entirely of natural and glazed brick, forming emblematic patterns. Brick was cheap and decorative and clearly had a promising future.

The start of the Renaissance in France has long been dated to the end of Charles VIII's minority (1491) and the first Italian campaign (1495). This is quite justifiable in that a change of style was most definitely evident, but the change was one of lifestyle and not, from the outset, a change in building style. Admittedly, construction of the château of Amboise was well advanced when the king set out. And what the French saw in Naples was a way of life that they wished to imitate. But Charles VIII's tastes were eclectic, and at Amboise the Flemish contribution is more apparent than the Italian. The Valois Renaissance was a last flaring up of the Flamboyant style illuminating the quest for something new.

This Renaissance was, moreover, essentially Ligerian; the kings had elected residence in the Loire Valley and the art of the aristocracy was at home there. One result of the change was the huge expansion of the court. Even after the reconstruction of Blois, Louis XII found it hard to accommodate the 322 chamberlains, major-domos, manservants and others who made up his personal retinue.

Châteaux too expanded, on an unparalleled scale. Two of the largest, Le Verger and Bonnivet, and the most modern, Bury, have almost entirely vanished. The construction of Bury began in 1511. It was built by Florimond Robertet, another

Château of Oiron. Gallery painted in the mid-16th century by Noël Jallier for Claude Gouffier, Master of the Horse. The series is one of the most important ensembles of the French Renaissance, and depicts scenes from the Iliad *and the* Aeneid.

financier, who might be termed Louis XII's prime minister. The regularity of the courtyard, the symmetry and rhythm of the façades and the integration of the *rampe-sur-rampe* staircase mark a turning point. The works of Louis XII and François I at Blois are astonishing in their magnificence. Innovation was the preserve of Cœur's followers: Robertet at Bury, Bohier at Chenonceaux and Berthelot at Azay-le-Rideau.

Azay-le-Rideau, which fortunately has survived, is the very pattern of the Ligerian châteaux built in the early years of François I's reign. It marks the slightly belated adoption of the innovations of Bury. Yet the most extraordinary château is in the king's territory: there seems to us no doubt that the project for Chambord drawn up in 1519 was the work of Leonardo da Vinci – a purely speculative project, the realization of which was the more problematic since Leonardo died as construction began. Leonardo's death marked the end of the halcyon days. François I was defeated and taken prisoner at Pavia (1525). On his liberation, he announced his intention of living in Paris. In fact, the decision benefited the châteaux of the Île-de-France rather than the Parisian palaces. The immediate effect was the condemnation of the great banker Jacques de Beaune-Semblançay who, prosecuted under the same heads as Jacques Cœur, was less fortunate and died on the scaffold. With him perished the network of Touraine financiers whose elevation had occurred under Louis XI. The Bohiers and the Berthelots had to hand over their châteaux to the king.

up on the lofty terraces which made its reputation, and which bear such a close resemblance to the Flamboyant belvederes of Jean de Berry. Forsaken, the Valley created a genre. At Villandry, Valençay, Beauregard, Villegongis, and Serrant, all of them châteaux built after 1530, we come across the arrangements imitated from Blois so typical of the Loire style: pilasters for each floor forming a grid with the double *cordon* string course between floors, and a multitude of details borrowed from the High Renaissance. Here and there a few innovations arose. Examples are Villesavin, where the single-story château surmounted by a roof space first appeared, and Villandry, where large, square-plan pavilions replaced the traditional round towers at the corners. It is no coincidence that these two châteaux had the same owner, the financier Jean Breton.

In interior decoration, the Loire Valley had not fallen behind the Île-de-Franc. The remarkable painted gallery at Oiron was conceived in the spirit of what was happening at Fontainebleau. At Beauregard, it was the royal artists from Fontainebleau or Saint-Germain who came to decorate the chapels, chambers and fireplaces.

In the 17th and 18th centuries, it was most often a matter of modernizing the 15th and 16th-century châteaux: knocking down a wing to open up a courtyard, rebuilding the main front, altering the interior layout to make the old châteaux habitable. The château at Le Lude is a good example of these transformations. At the same date, Gabriel and Soufflot, the most noted architects of the

Building in the Loire Valley continued for some years under its own momentum. Chambord had been mismanaged, and almost all the building work took place after Pavia. It was then that this airy village sprang

time, transformed the château of Menars for the Marquise de Pompadour and her brother and heir, the Marquis de Marigny. But the great achievement of this period was the gardens.

One château of the period stands out. Despite the alterations carried out during the 18th century, Cheverny remains a fine example of the château architecture from the first decades of the 17th century. Nonetheless, only the château of Richelieu deserves a mention in a general history of architecture. And from the 17th century on, Richelieu was already considered remote and provincial. La Fontaine said of the town that Richelieu sought to create around his castle that "it would soon achieve the glory of being the finest village in the universe." Richelieu should have "chosen another spot ... but the desire to glorify the place of his birth obliged him to build around the room where he was born." (Letter from La Fontaine to his wife, 5 September 1663.) The remark held for Loire Valley as a whole. It had been occupied since ancient times, and could not suddenly be abandoned. A number of dynasties maintained their roots there and venerated the places that gave them their names.

This was again evident in the 19th century when the great aristocratic families of the Restoration returned to the land, leading to a rash of neo-Renaissance châteaux in Anjou. They are found also in the geographical region known as the Sologne, the southern part of the Orléanais area, between the Loire and the Cher, and northern part of Berry, where systematic reforestation and the

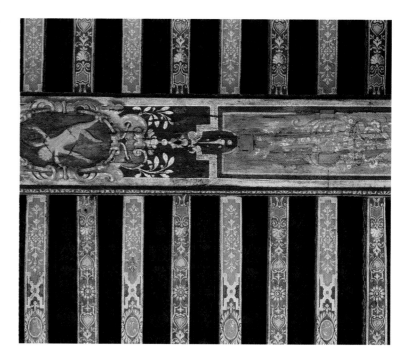

vicinity of Paris were a strong attraction for huntsmen. The repopulation of the Sologne was more varied than that of Anjou – captains of industry arrived there along with the railways. One of the most important of these Sologne hunting lodges, constructed in the style of Chambord and twelve miles from the royal château, is Bon-Hôtel, which dates from the end of the 19th century.

The Loire Valley style was not confined to France, as Waddesdon Manor shows; it spread throughout Europe and the world. But that could be matter for another book again.

Detail of a floor at Cheverny. When the structure of beams and joists is visible, the floor is known as a French-style floor. It was a type, often painted, that gradually went out of fashion in French architecture in the mid-17th century.

LEFT-HAND PAGE:
Château d'Oiron: the fireplace in the gallery.

AINAY-LE-VIEIL

The accident of alphabetical order brings us into the Loire Valley via the upper valley of the Cher and the ancient province of Bourbonnais, far from the great châteaux of the royal demesne.

The château of Ainay-le-Vieil is situated in flat land with no natural defenses. It was probably built over the remains of a Gallo-Roman farm and villa, which was fortified at a later date. Today it consists of a polygonal *enceinte* with round towers at the corners. Within the *enceinte*, its back to the curtain wall, stands a house comprising two wings at right angles with a stair tower at the center.

When were the curtain walls built? We can only guess. The castellany is mentioned in the late 12th century as belonging to the Lords of Bourbon. From the mid-12th century it belonged to the powerful Sully family. At the end of the 14th century, it passed into the hands of the Culan family. The bulk of the *enceinte* may well date from the mid-14th century, when the provinces of Berry and Bourbonnais were under attack from the English.

THIS PAGE:
Kneeling portraits of Claude de Bigny and Gilbert de Bigny. The figures of father and son match those of their wives (preceding page) on the facing wall of the chapel.

OPPOSITE:
The chapel, with 17th-century painting; the stained glass is by the master glazier Jean Lescuyer (first half of 16th century).

In the great drawing room is a fireplace with the arms of France and the monogram LA, for Louis XII and Anne de Bretagne.

On the basis of dates and coats of arms inscribed on the house, the construction is attributed to three generations of the Bigny family: Charles de Chevenon, Lord of Bigny, who bought the château in 1467, his son Claude and his grandson Gilbert. But monograms and coats of arms can be added; at best, they date only the work which bears them. It is quite possible that the house was built by the famous Jacques Cœur, Charles VII's treasurer, who bought Ainay in 1443. In the same year, scarcely ten leagues away, Jacques Cœur bought the land on which he later built the most remarkable town house of the 15th century. Ainay's Flamboyant Gothic is certainly comparable to that of the Bourges town house. The barley-sugar columns on the upper floors of the stair tower are reminiscent of those in the neighboring château of Meillant, which dates from the first decade of the 16th century. The large chimney of Ainay is of similar date: it bears the monograms L and A, for Louis XII and Anne de Bretagne, who visited Claude de Bigny at Ainay. The keystone of the chapel is decorated with the arms of Claude de Bigny and his wife Jacqueline de L'Hospital, and Gilbert de Bigny and his wife Charlotte Lorfèvre. The kneeling figures of these two couples, painted in the 1530s on the chapel walls, were left intact when the remarkable painted decoration of the chapel was carried out in 1609. Recent restoration work has brought the latter to light under the 19th century paintwork.

In the second half of the 19th century, the Marquis Jean-Baptiste de Bligny undertook substantial "restoration" work. The two loggias on the façades, clearly inspired by the loggia façade at the château of Blois, may be 19th-century additions. The dormers themselves must have been remodeled.

AMBOISE

The château in which Charles VIII was born in 1431 had been confiscated from the Amboise family. After his marriage to the Duchess Anne de Bretagne in 1491, he began an almost total reconstruction, which was unfinished when, in 1498, he hit his head on the lintel of a low doorway and died.

Charles VIII first restored the old château, which stood at the rocky end of the spur overlooking the town and the Loire. The new château was not built on that site but inside the former outer bailey, doubtless because the promontory was far wider at that point. The two main buildings were built along

On the left, the Charles VIII
wing overlooking the town and
the Loire; on the right, the Louis
XII – François I wing facing the
garden. The former was built for
Charles VIII in the 1490s, while
the latter was begun by Louis XII
and completed by François I
around 1520.

OPPOSITE:
In the foreground is the Loire;
above it is the town; above the
town are the Charles VIII wing of
the château with its garden (left),
and the huge, round Minim
Tower (center), which contains a
ramp allowing mounted riders to
ascend from river level to the
plateau on which the château is
built.

the steep sides of the spur; one on the Loire side, the other, known as the Seven Virtues building after the statues of the Virtues with which it was decorated, over the other cliff. The *piano nobile* on the Loire side, which has survived 19th-century restoration work more or less intact, is entirely taken up by a single great room. The Seven Virtues building no longer exists, but its *piano nobile* contained an apartment for the king and one for the queen symmetrically arranged on opposite sides of the same room. This suggests that the building on the Loire side was reserved for receptions and the exercise of sovereignty, while the Seven Virtues building was for private life.

On the courtyard side, at right angles to the building facing the Loire, was another dwelling for the king. This was perhaps begun by Charles VIII and completed by François I.

The functions of the buildings, which would of course have varied, especially on a site where construction was still proceeding, is not obvious. Each of the buildings had (and still has) direct access from the valley below via a vaulted spiral ramp (which can be ascended by carriage) enclosed in a large round tower. This tended to reinforce the complementary nature of (or rivalry between) the two buildings, and must therefore have had a symbolic value. In the broader part of

The chapel stands at the edge of
the plateau on which the
château is built, on the cliff
opposite that overlooking the
town. The wings that linked it
with the residential blocks were
demolished. It was begun in
1491, at the beginning of
Charles VIII's reign, and
finished in 1496, the year of the
first Italian war. It bears no sign
of Italian influence. The names
of the artists who built it testify
to their northern origin, viz.
Corneille of Nesve and Casin of
Utrecht. On the lintel of the
doorway are the legends of St.
Christopher and St. Hubert.

OPPOSITE:
Great hall of the Charles VIII
wing. It was completely
remodeled in the 19th century.

the promontory once stood the 11th century collegiate church of Saint-Florentin; there was also a garden.

Very few signs of Italian art can be traced in this château built by the king who launched the first Italian war, and perhaps even these were added by his successor. In fact, the main features of the building had been decided before Charles VIII left to invade Naples (1494) and he died soon after his return in 1496. The only artist among those brought from Italy whose activity is documented is Pacello da

Interior of the chapel of the château.

RIGHT:
Great hall of the Charles VIII wing. It was completely remodeled in the 19th century.

Mercogliano, and the Amboise gardens may have been laid out before the arrival of this architecteur. By contrast, the famous spiral ramps may have been modeled on a similar tower at Urbino, whose reputation probably reached France before the expedition reached Italy.

Italian rather than Flemish workers constructed the Flamboyant chapel. According to Philippe de Commynes, Charles VIII "brought together all the fine things that had been praised to him, wherever they had been seen, in France, Italy or Flanders." Perhaps he sought a return to the florid style of the châteaux of Charles V and his brothers, a style that war and thrift had precluded during the last three reigns. Louis XI, the frugal father, built Langeais. Charles, the prodigal son, built Amboise with an extrovert façade that opens out in its upper part like a château by duc Jean de Berry.

Yet the great balcony, with its wrought iron railings and of French windows, is a great innovation, and provides a pointer to the future.

The Minim Tower contains a
[spiral] ramp by which
horsemen can ride up from the
Loire banks to the château. The
Hurtault tower on the cliffside
opposite serves the same
purpose.

The two towers were begun on
the orders of Charles VIII.
Italianate features appear only
in the upper part of the Hurtault
tower, but the two towers
probably derive from the mid-
15th century rampe cavalière
at the palace of Urbino.

ANGERS

with the wall in the late 16th century. Louis succeeded his father Louis VIII in 1226 while still a minor, so it seems likely that the regent, Blanche de Castille, initiated the work.

In 1246, in accordance with the will of Louis VIII, Louis IX gave up the county of Anjou to his brother Charles, the founder of the first House of Anjou of the Capetian dynasty; it later carried the Angevin name as far abroad as Sicily and Hungary. Anjou had been seized by Philippe Auguste from the King of England in 1205, but it was still under threat from its powerful neighbors. The new construction was thus not a residence but a defensive castle. We do not know exactly how this vast space of 6.17 acres was filled, but the main buildings must have stood along the banks of the Maine; the bailey with its round towers does not extend along the river bank.

The House of Anjou – now of the Valois dynasty – endeavored to fill the space thus protected. The Duchy of Anjou had been created in 1360 by Jean II le Bon for his son Louis I, and in 1373 Louis commissioned the famous tapestry of the *Apocalypse* from the painter Hennequin de Bruges and the Parisian tapestry weaver Nicolas Bataille. This is one of the masterpieces of French tapestry-making, and is still to be seen in the castle.

Louis II, son of Louis I, and Yolande d' Aragon had the chapel (1405–1412) and the royal apartments built. The chapel is a *sainte chapelle*, a name given to those churches that

External view of walls.

The enormous 600-meter perimeter wall, constructed in shale, sandstone and granite, was built in the 1230s, the first decade of the reign of Louis IX. It comprises seventeen towers which originally rose 35 feet above the level of the wall; they were brought level

View of barbican through a gateway in the perimeter wall.

enshrined a relic of the Passion, in this case a splinter of the fragment of the True Cross acquired by Louis IX and shared among the royal princes. The dwelling could claim to be a royal one as the duke was also King of Sicily and of Aragon.

The scale of the buildings made the château of Angers predominant among the duke's Loire Valley territories, which included Saumur. The additions by René, the son of Louis II who became famous, indeed almost popular, as Good King René, "King of Sicily" after its loss, are more modest. These buildings seem to have been scattered randomly around the bailey, a disposition typical of fortresses primarily defined by their fortified perimeter.

It was as heir to King Réné that Louis XI recovered Anjou. Thereafter, only the ducal title survived, handed down to the younger sons of the House of France without the accompanying territorial jurisdiction.

ARGY

The château of Argy consists of wings around a rectangular courtyard, with angle towers. The large square tower called the keep was originally the gatehouse. The wing linking this keep to the Brillac Tower, the large round tower, contains two superposed open galleries. The adjacent wing includes an open gallery on the first floor and a large hall on the second. The façade is covered with a scattering of ermines, fleurs-de-lis and interlaced initials which remind us that Charles de Brillac, the château's owner, was Louis XII's major domo. The ermines are clearly a tribute to Anne de Bretagne, the Queen. The

ABOVE:
*Courtyard with Brillac Tower at
the rear.*

OPPOSITE:
Gallery facing the courtyard.

dormers in the wing are 19th-century additions, like the third wing and the last two towers. The fourth wing, which enclosed the courtyard, was demolished in the 18th century when the outhouses were being built. The two gallery wings, the keep and the Brillac Tower are, in essence, the work of Charles de Brillac, who died in Milan in 1509.

However, work may have been started by one of his ancestors (the Brillacs acquired Argy in the mid-15th century), and Charles may thus have reused some of the medieval buildings.

AZAY-LE-RIDEAU

Azay-le-Rideau was constructed in the Renaissance style for Gilles Berthelot, Mayor of Tours and Treasurer-General of the Finances of France. The main building and return wing were completed between 1518 and 1527. Unluckily for Berthelot, he became embroiled in a financial scandal and was forced to leave the country, whereupon the king promptly confiscated the château. Had it not been for this unhappy event, it is likely that the second return wing and entry wing, both of which were inherited from the medieval castle, would have been rebuilt in the same style. (They were demolished in the 17th century.) The visitor would then have been able to appreciate the symmetry of the main building and its famous central staircase. This symmetry was broken when the courtyard façade was extended. The mistake was compounded when, in the 19th century, a tower and a turret were built onto the ends of the added wing and the main building to create the illusion of a completed château. Azay's most remarkable feature is its internal staircase. Though inspired by Châteaudun, it consists of straight flights. These features were found in other pioneering châteaux, but Azay-le-Rideau's is the oldest surviving example.

Rear façade of château

THIS PAGE:
*Courtyard façade. The
staircase occupies the two
central bays, as usual with the
dog-leg staircases in fashion in
the 16th century: two straight
flights separated by a wall
make a 180-degree turn at
each floor and at intermediate
landings. The intermediate
landings have loggias opening
onto the courtyard.*

OPPOSITE:
*Entrance door of staircase and
openings of the first
intermediate landing. Between
the two levels are the
salamander of François I and
the ermine of Claude de
France. In the 16th century,
private individuals would
display royal emblems on their
homes.*

Vault of a staircase and landing. The vaults are typical of the transition from the Gothic technique of arches to the Italianate style of flat ceilings and narrative scenes. The pilasters with a diamond in the middle and two half-diamonds at the ends are French Renaissance borrowings from Italian art.

Salamander of François I.

The great hall.

Delinquents at Azay-le-Rideau

Less useful in times of peace, fortifications remained prestigious. Gilles Berthelot had no mind to deny himself fortifications when reconstructing Azay-le-Rideau. He had to justify his request to the king, emphasizing the danger from delinquents robbing the neighborhood and attacking the village: "Because of the great throng of traffic there, bad characters are found day and night, public thieves, footpads and other vagabonds, evildoers committing affray, disputes, thefts, larcenies, outrages, extortions and sundry other evils and calamities, because the said village is not enclosed with gates or walls, and they can then withdraw into the great forests of Chinon and other woods."

As with most contemporary roofs, the roofs at Azay-le-Rideau are of the raised-wall type. The façade walls which carry the roof frame are raised above the upper story, allowing the roof space to be occupied. The windows take the form of dormers and are set partly into the raised wall and partly into the slope of the roof.

BELOW:
Extract from Monuments historiques *(1904) showing a section of the main house and the courtyard façade of the right wing. The section shows the arrangement of the dog-leg staircase.*

OPPOSITE:
At the back, the courtyard façade of the right wing; in the foreground, the end of the main house. The end was remodeled in the 19th century following the demolition of the left wing of the courtyard.

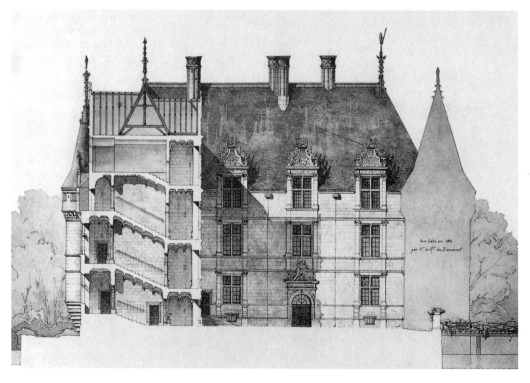

LA BASTIE D'URFÉ

On the right is the wing with the large flight of steps, at the rear the main house. In the middle of the ground floor is the doorway of the chapel, and to the right of it the arcades of the grotto.

The River Lignon flows down from the Monts du Forez in the Massif Central joining the Loire as it meets the plain. In passing, it filled the moats (now filled in) of La Bastie, which came into the Urfé family's possession in the 13th century. (The word *bastie* is derived from the Old French verb *bastir*, meaning "to build", as are "bastion" and

"Bastille".) The Urfé family remained stead-fastly loyal to the king and assumed the office of bailiff (*bailli*) of the Forez region as a quasi-hereditary appointment. The other Forez families that prospered during the Renaissance – the Robertets, the Albons and the Gouffiers – built their châteaux as near as possible to the royal residences. Arthus and Claude Gouffier,

One of the oldest preserved examples of the fashion for little pleasure temples erected in gardens.

for example, built the château of Oiron. By contrast, Claude d'Urfé, who carved out a brilliant career in the service of François I and Henry II, devoted himself to embellishing remote La Bastie. His attentions changed a humble rustic castle into one of the most remarkable buildings of the French Renaissance. Early in the following century, the

Details of the steps. The meaning of the figures is not clear, though figures of Abundance and Hercules struggling with the Nemean lion have been identified. But the mystery is intentional, as is proven by the enigmatic inscription on the sphinx: "Sphingem habe domi" (lit. "have the sphinx in the house"). A liberal translation might be "the secret is reserved for the initiated."

The grotto. Originally, it contained four large statues depicting the seasons. The decoration is made of sand, pebbles, colored stones and shells.

Lignon, on whose banks Claude's descendant Honoré d'Urfé set his tales of bucolic love, entered court and drawing rooms with *L'Astrée* (1607–1624). Honoré's story of the shepherdess Astrée and her lover Céladon became a bestseller of *préciosité*.

Claude d'Urfé was raised at court, and was a mere boy when he took part in the Italian wars. In 1535, François I made him bailiff of Forez, and in 1546 made him a royal representative of the Council of Trent, where the reformation of the Catholic Church was decided. In 1548, Henri II appointed him ambassador to the Holy See, only to recall him in 1550 to make him tutor to the Dauphin, the future François II, a position he retained until his death in 1558. In this post, the highly cultured Claude d'Urfé collaborated with the illustrious scholars and poets Jacques Amyot and Joachim Du Bellay.

Two personal events have left visible traces on the buildings of La Bastie. Firstly, Claude's ten-year marriage to Jeanne de Balsac (1532–1542), whose J interlaced with two Cs testifies to the fidelity of her husband and widower, and secondly Claude's admission in 1549 to the royal Order of St. Michael, the collar of which was thereafter included in his coat of arms.

The château grew round a rectangular tower, originally closed. Claude d'Urfé's main initiative was to double the right wing by adding two superposed open galleries, with a large flight of steps giving access to the upper gallery. Claude also equipped the back wing with a grotto, that is to say a room decorated with rocaille work, and leading on from this, a chapel. These works are usually dated to 1548, during his absence in Italy, but the date is certain only for the chapel. The other additions must be pre-1549, because the Urfé arms appear on them without the Order of St.

THIS PAGE:
Basement.

OPPOSITE:
The decoration of the chapel was dispersed in 1874. The remarkable marquetry panels that covered the lower parts are now in the Metropolitan Museum of New York, while the stained glass windows are in a private collection. Happily, however, the altar and paintings by Girolamo Siciolante are back in place.

Michael. On stylistic grounds, they look some ten or even twenty years earlier.

The arcades of the lower gallery, which form a return in front of the grotto, are clumsy but pleasing imitations of 15th-century Italian work, reminiscent of those built for Anne de Beaujeu at the château of Moulins in the late 15th century. Moulins was the first Ligerian location to exhibit Italian influences, and is close to La Bastie.

In contrast, the chapel, with its doorway onto the courtyard, dates from the 1540s, and is a Renaissance masterpiece. Its interior fittings were dispersed in 1874. The paintings have been restored to their places, but the inlaid paneling is now in the Metropolitan Museum, New York, and the stained glass windows, dating from 1557, are in private hands.

The paintings are by Girolamo Siciolante, a pupil of Perino del Vaga, who was nurtured on paintings by Raphael and Michelangelo and is mentioned in Vasari's *Lives of the Painters*. They were commissioned when Claude d'Urfé was ambassador to the Vatican. The woodwork was similarly commissioned from Fra Damiano (Antoniolo di Zambelli), a specialist in marquetry still life and architecture. Fragments of the floor tiles, made by the Rouen workshop of Masseot Abaquesnes, are preserved at Écouen, Rouen

*Altar of the chapel.
Above, the front of the altar,
depicting Noah's sacrifice and
the end of the Flood. Below, one
of the sides, showing the
Israelites crossing the Red Sea.
The author of these mid-16th-
century bas-reliefs has not been
identified.*

Painting of the Annunciation, from the chapel.

and the Louvre. The stucco work on the vault may be the work of an artist brought from Fontainebleau.

At the junction of the wings stand two bastion towers bearing the date 1555. The left wing of the courtyard probably dates from the same period. Yet its division into a suite of identical quarters, each with separate access to the court, resembles the private barracks erected during the Wars of Religion. Claude's son Jacques d'Urfé took an active part in these wars.

The little round temple can probably be attributed to Claude d'Urfé. It is the sole relic of the gardens and one of the oldest garden structures in France.

Paintings in the chapel.
OPPOSITE:
Abraham preparing to sacrifice
Isaac.

ABOVE:
Abraham blessed by
Melchisedech.

Room with decoration from the
mid-17th century.
Gallery in right hand wing
dating from the 15th century. It
was the only room decorated
subsequent to the major works
undertaken in the mid-16th
century.
Note unusual positioning of the
joists.

BAUGÉ

In the 11th century, the site was occupied by a castle situated between two streams, both tributaries of the Loire. Nearby was a village now called Vieil Baugé. Burnt down in 1436 by the English, the castle was rebuilt by René of Anjou on the original motte, at the base of which the town of Baugé has grown up. In 1454, its reconstruction was entrusted to Guillaume Robin, "master of works for the King of Sicily". René, Duke of Anjou, Bar and Lorraine, Count of Provence and King of Naples and Sicily, had in fact lost his kingdom in 1442. These titles were in addition to his claim to the kingdoms of Hungary and Jerusalem. The château was already partly habitable for René's stay in 1462–63, and in 1467 Baugé became his principal residence. In 1471, René left the duchy for good, as Louis XI had reclaimed it for the kingdom; he retired to Provence, where his memory is still revered.

The main building is the only surviving part of a château whose fortified perimeter encompassed courtyards, gardens and outbuildings. Entrance was via a tower that has not survived but which formerly rested against the town wall. The main building thus commanded a view to the north-west over the town and over the enclosed area to the south-east, an orientation traditionally preferred. This made the façade with the stair towers the main one.

The larger stair tower serves a long main building with a suite of reception rooms. At the end are the private apartments, where the house is extended on the town side by a large square pavilion. The apartments are reached via a second tower, forming a pair with the first and containing a second spiral staircase

The chapel.

OPPOSITE:
The façades over the town. The pavilion contains the apartments, while the long building contains the great reception rooms.

and, on the upper floor, an oratory.

In the enclosed area was a chapel and the garden no doubt contained some of the amenities that made the reputation of the Angevin residences of King René. René delighted in the vogue for *maisons des champs*, modest manors preferred by the great lords to their imposing fortresses. It was a fashion that developed in the middle of the century with the return of peace. For example, in 1454 Guillaume Robin, the architect of Baugé, created the manor house of La Menitré for King René.

The château of Baugé belongs to another genre altogether. It is more closed than open, more wall than openwork; ultimately, less

Vaulting of the great staircase. It is built of eight three-quarter ribbed vaults.

modern than the châteaux of Berry, where, nearly a century earlier, duc Jean had raised great expanses of openwork in Flamboyant Gothic, during another period of peace.

There is, moreover, nothing here to remind us that King René was one of the first in his Provence territory to commission work from Italian sculptors.

In the 15th century, the roof space contained important rooms. In the attic in the foreground is a room of which a large window and fireplace are visible; in the roof space in the background are two floors plus chimney.

René d'Anjou

In 1474, King Louis XI annexed Anjou and forced his nephew René of Anjou to withdraw to Provence.

"The tender-hearted and easy-going King of Sicily (*René*) relinquished his duchy of Anjou. What pen could describe the sorrows and complaints of the people of Anjou on seeing themselves deprived of so watchful a guardian, protector of the country, preserver of the Church, maintainer of the nobility, defender of the commons, lover of peace, sustainer of the poor, chivalrous guide and support of ladies and demoiselles, incorruptible administrator of justice ..."

As to the person of this prince, he was very handsome, tall and upright, with a fine chest and well made in all his limbs, but a wound he received at the capture of Barrois had marked his face somewhat. And although he was a very prudent man and well versed in arms, he was never fortunate in war. In his character he was considered a just man and never did anyone wrong. In humanity, religion, liberality, nobility and courage he surpassed all the kings that had reigned in Sicily before him ...

And was ever town more amazed than was Angers after he was gone which was while he resided there, the *fons et origo* of all pleasure and rejoicing and the most honored house of France. And the great love and vehement affection that the people of Anjou bore this good king is clear to see; for no decent house in Angers (except those built since) is without his arms or some words of his mottos."

Jean de Bourdigné, *Histoire agrégative des annales et chroniques d'Anjou*, 1529

BEAUGENCY

Towering over the château at Beaugency is a huge 11th-century keep. It was probably built for Ralph I, seigneur of Beaugency from 1090 to 1130. Ralph was an independent lord who dared to support the enemies of the French king.

The square keep stands at 117 feet high, although the top two floors were added in the 13th or 14th century. The original building was motted, that is to say, buried to a height of twenty feet and protected by a double perimeter wall. The only way into the lowest room was through the room above it, which could itself be reached only by a ladder. In 1281, Ralph sold the domain to the King of France, who ceded it in 1379 to the Duke of Orléans. In 1441, Beaugency became the property of the famous Jean de Dunois, the bastard of Orléans. Under his direction a number of improvements were made, notably to the keep, where opening windows and chimneys were added and internal walls rearranged. He is probably also responsible for the construction of the neighboring small manor house.

During the Wars of Religion in the 16th century, the keep was badly damaged and has since fallen into ruin.

THIS PAGE AND OPPOSITE:
The keep.

BEAUREGARD

Beauregard's exceptionally interesting interior decoration was commissioned by Jean Du Thier, Lord of Menars, Secretary of State to Henri II and friend of the poet Ronsard; Du Their bought the château in 1545, and built most of the surviving castle.

The chapel frescoed by Niccolò dell'Abate has disappeared, but the frescoes on the fireplace of the royal chamber are still to be seen and are reminiscent of the style of that celebrated Fontainebleau painter.

The valuable paneling in the Cabinet des Grelots (Snowdrop Room), dotted with the heraldic snowdrops of Jean Du Thier, is the work of an Italian artist working in Fontainebleau, the equally famous Scibec di Carpi. The allegorical paintings are perhaps by Niccolò dell'Abate himself.

The Great Gallery has preserved only one fireplace in the Italian style from Du Thier's time. Its principal feature is the remarkable decoration commissioned by Paul Ardier, Comptroller of Wars and Treasurer, who purchased Beauregard in 1617, and his son Paul, President of the Paris *Chambre des comptes*. The Delft floor tiling was acquired in 1627, and laid by Paul in 1646; he also collected portraits of the famous to decorate the gallery. Such galleries were very popular during the 17th century. A notable predecessor was that of the Palais Royal, dating from the 1630s.

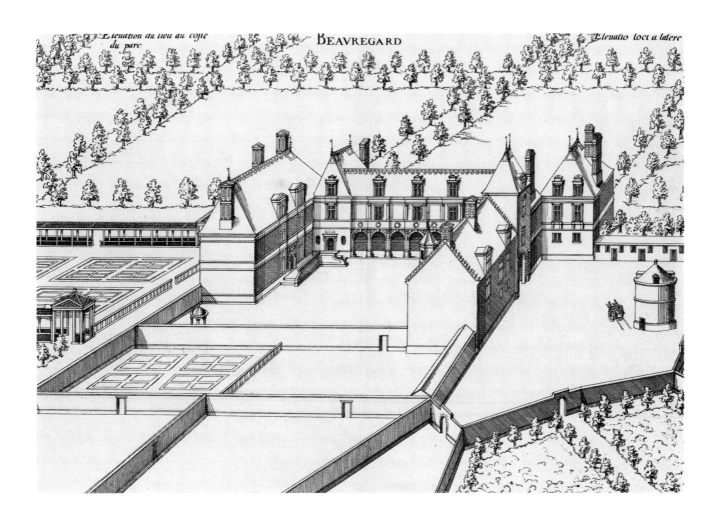

Eleuation du lieu du cofte du parc

BEAVREGARD

Eleuatio loci a latere

Beauregard

"The building is not large, but it is dainty and as neatly arranged as one could desire. Like the building, everything is agreeable and pretty; as is the garden," writes Jacques Androuet Du Cerceau in *Les plus excellents bastiments de France* (1579).

And, indeed, Beauregard reflects perfectly the refined taste and cultivation of the man who had it built, Jean Du Thier. Du Thier was a friend of the humanists and particularly of Ronsard, who encouraged his book-loving tastes:

With coin you recompense the books
Whose lives have borne the centuries down;
Upon their spine as guide are seen
Great names: Pindar. Simonides.
With these the castle stands adorned
Your beauregard thus more refined.

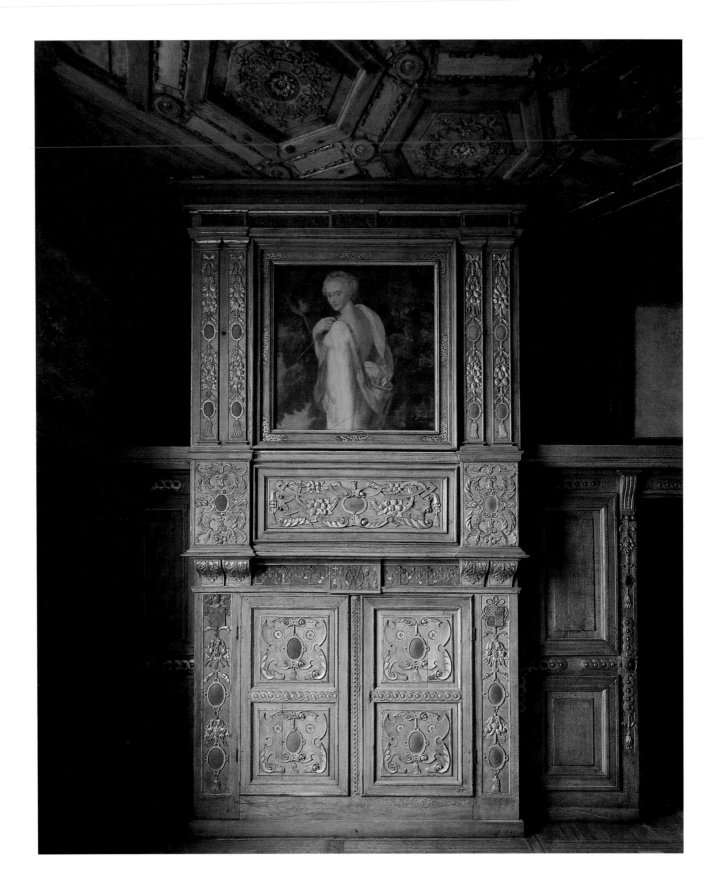

OPPOSITE:
The Snowdrop Room.

THIS PAGE:
Gallery decorated in 1646 with 300 portraits of famous men and women. This type of decoration, often used to flatter royalty and glorify the ancestral line of the owner, was very fashionable in the first half of the 17th century, but few examples have survived. The floor is covered with Delft tiles representing an army.

Gallery of Fame. The white marble fireplace is an original part of the gallery created in the mid-16th century. The lower part of the paneling may also partly date back to this period. Most of it, however, is 17th-century. Intepretation is difficult, though the porcupine of Louis XII and salamander of François I are recognizable at the top.

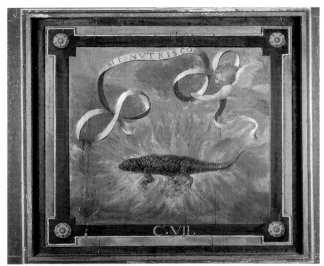

BLOIS

Loggia façade, facing the town.

The square at the entrance to Blois is the former bailey of a fortress built on the tip of a rocky spur naturally defended on three sides and cut off from the rest of the plateau by a moat. The "barred spur" (as this kind of fortified site is called) had been occupied long before the Merovingian *castrum* is recorded.

The counts of Blois are documented from the late 6th century on. Early in the Capetian era, they already numbered among the most powerful lords of the kingdom. Their descendants inherited the county of Champagne and kingdom of Navarre.

All that remains of the bailey is the Foix

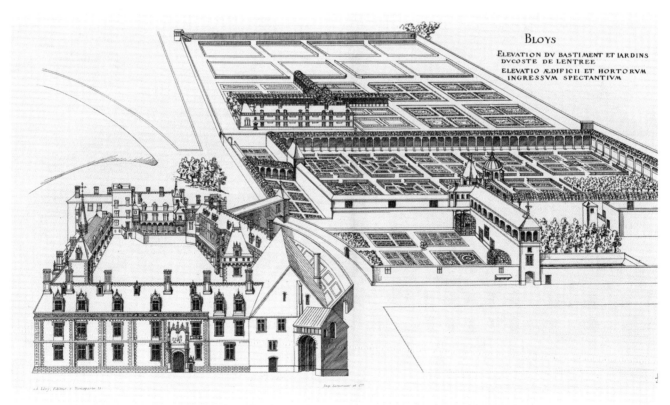

Above, the Loggia Façade, from Les plus excellents bastiments de France (1579) by Jacques Androuet Du Cerceau. On the right, a round tower from the former bailey is enclosed in the façade. On the extreme right, a medieval house, which was replaced by the Gaston d'Orléans wing. Below, [an aerial view] the château and its gardens, from the entrance side.

Tower, now standing by itself to the south, part of the enceinte over which the François I wing was built. The States Room in the northern corner twice accommodated the States General of the kingdom. It is a rare example of a large feudal hall from the early 13th century.

In 1391, the county of Blois was purchased by Louis, the brother of King Charles VI, who became Duke of Orléans the following year. His son Charles, the poet, taken prisoner by the English at Azincourt, retired to Blois after being freed. Nothing appears to have survived of the – no doubt considerable – transformations that he oversaw. Charles's son Louis, who became Duke of Orléans in 1465, brought the Valois–Orléans line to the throne in 1498, and left to his successor François I (1515) a château that remained royal until Louis XIII gave it to his brother Gaston, along with the title of Duke of Orléans.

As it stands today, the château is an irregular quadrilateral bordered by buildings traditionally called the Charles d'Orléans wing, the Louis XII wing, the François I wing and the Gaston d'Orléans wing. The four corners are at cardinal points. This is too common an arrangement in contemporary châteaux to be accidental. It may have been imposed by the constraints of the site, but equally the site may have been preferred because it permitted such an arrangement. The side enjoying the best aspect was thus the one which looked out over the Loire. But, oddly enough, this front is only occupied by the lower wing named after Charles d'Orléans, onto which is built the

Saint-Calais Chapel. In the 18th and 19th centuries, the chapel and wing were shortened; formerly they closed the courtyard in. Thus the Loire aspect, where one would expect to find the main building, is incomplete. But the last word in the history of this much debated château has yet to be written.

The wing whose construction was long attributed to Charles d'Orléans is nowadays ascribed to Louis XII. It seems likely to have been integral with the choir of the chapel, which was consecrated in 1508.

ABOVE:
Courtyard façade of the Gaston d'Orléans wing.

OPPOSITE:
The entrance gateway, with its equestrian statue of Louis XII, was remodeled in the 19th century.

THIS PAGE:
*Courtyard façade and staircase
of the François I wing.*

OPPOSITE:
*Detail of the staircase of the
François I wing.*

If we believe that Louis d'Orléans waited until he had inherited the throne and married his predecessor's widow, Anne de Bretagne, before building the 'Louis XII' wing, it follows that, during the 30 years when he was only Duke of Orléans, nothing was changed, or nothing has survived of the changes. In fact, the Louis XII wing is probably just a reconstruction of a medieval building, augmented by two spiral staircases, one of which is quite remarkable. The wing is crossed by a passage leading to the courtyard, yet it has none of the defensive works usual near entrances. We are told that this modern monarch was thus setting his lords an example and demonstrating that his authority need

no longer fear surprise attack. But what of the protection afforded by the courtyard (now the square) that stood in front of the Louis XII wing?

The style of decoration is still almost entirely Gothic, with the exception of a few Italianizing motifs probably executed by French craftsmen. Admittedly, before leading the French into Italy, Louis had taken part in his predecessor's Neapolitan expedition (1494–5), but we know that the Italian style was not introduced before 1508 at Gaillon, the avant-garde château of the Cardinal of Amboise, Louis XII's all-powerful minister.

It was probably Louis XII who ordered gardens to be laid out at the foot of the spur –

Staircase of the Louis XII wing.

one of them is mentioned in 1470. However, the creation of the Great Garden dates from 1499, when land was bought for it. The work is attributed to Pacello da Mercogliano, a "gardener" brought back from the first expedition. The Italian did not tear up the traditional French garden but introduced Mediterranean species and an ingenious system of irrigation. The only surviving features of this garden are what is was probably the first French orangery, and the pavilion named after Anne de Bretagne, the oldest folly in France.

The François I wing, begun in the first months of his reign, prior to the victory at Marignano which opened the way to Italy, formed part of a project whose fate seems to have been sealed by 1517–18. At that date François had brought Leonardo da Vinci back to France; Leonardo was set to work on his design for the château at Chambord – a

remarkable and innovative scheme quite unlike the Blois wing. The "Blesois order" of superposed pilasters and double horizontal *cordon* molding is so called because Blois made it fashionable throughout the Loire Valley, but it did not originate at Blois.

The open spiral staircase, the outstanding example of the Valois taste for this feature, is anything but a pioneering work. It is in a stair-tower, whereas the mid-15th century spiral stairs at Châteaudun were wholly integrated, establishing the convention that prevailed thereafter. The most modern and Italian façade is the Loggia's. Contemporary

with the Vatican loggias by Bramante and Raphael, it is probably an imitation of them. The Loggia façade looked over the gardens, which the town slowly swallowed up. Thus, despite its north-westerly aspect, it became the king's quarters. We know that he was still living there in the late 16th century. The plan which François Mansart presented to Gaston d'Orléans in 1634 was a total reconstruction which would have swallowed up all the 16th-century buildings. These were partly and indirectly saved by Louis XIV. Until 1638, Gaston d'Orléans spent money as only the heir to the throne could; the birth of his

LEFT:
Staircase of the François I wing.

RIGHT:
Staircase of the Orléans wing with drum opening into a second cupola.

ABOVE:
States Room.

nephew Louis shattered his hopes of the throne.

The wing built between 1634 and 1638 is a masterpiece of French architecture, though it meant the destruction of the Perche aux Bretons, one of the oddest parts of the château, built in the early 16th or late 15th century, and now known only from engravings. Mansart's staircase in the new wing occupies its full depth and is roofed by an openwork beneath a solid cupola. In the art of effects, Mansart had nothing to learn from his Italian contemporary, Bernini. Thus, as La Fontaine observes, the château of Blois "was built in several stages, one part under François I, the other under one of his predecessors. There is a main house in the modern style that Monsieur [Gaston d'Orléans] began. These three bits do not, thank God, have any symmetry and have no connection or conformity with each other." (Letter to his wife). After La Fontaine's visit, nothing remains to mention but the considerable work carried out by Jacques Félix Duban in the mid-19th century. It can scarcely be called a restoration, but it produced notable neo-Renaissance interior decoration.

**The poet Charles, Duke of Orléans,
at his château of Blois**

Charles d'Orléans (...) was almost fifty when he was finally released from his long imprisonment. No longer troubled by the cares of public affairs or his princely rank, he led a comfortable, indeed leisurely existence in his pleasant castle at Blois on the banks of the Loire, surrounded by his small circle of gentlemen of letters and parasitic poets. For the remainder of his days, he cultivated the image of the charming but disillusioned man of the world, (...) enjoying a life without illusions, prepared for death and desiring only "a roaring hearth in winter and plenty to drink in summer" – along with good company and lively conversation. For all the rest of the world he cared not a jot, and asked no more of it than he gave.

Gustave Lanson (1857–1934)
Histoire de la littérature française

The murder of the Duke of Guise at the château of Blois

Henri, Duke of Guise, called Scarface, head of the Catholic League, gradually established himself as an ever more powerful figure in the kingdom, in the face of a weakened royal power. He demanded that the States General be recalled and claimed for himself the post of Lieutenant General of the Realm [the king's deputy]. Fearing for his person, Henri III escaped from Paris, but could not prevent the States General meeting at Blois.

In 1588, the king decided to eliminate his rival:

"It was nearly eight o'clock when the Duc de Guise was wakened by his valets, telling him the king was ready to leave; he quickly rose and dressed in a costume of gray satin, left to go to the council and soon after he was seated:

"I'm cold," he said, "I have pains in my chest; let us have a fire!"

Summoned by the king to the old study, he made his way thither. There he was beset with dagger blows.

The Duc exclaiming at each blow:

"Hey! Friends! Hey!"

and when he feels de Suriac's dagger in his rump, he shrieked:

"Mercy!"

And though he had his sword entangled in his cloak and his legs pinned, such was his strength, that he drew them from one end of the room to the other, to the foot of the bed, where he fell."

François Miron, *Relation de la mort de messieurs le Duc et le Cardinal de Guyse*

BON HÔTEL

Bon Hôtel is one of the most spectacular of the hunting lodges constructed in the second half of the 19th century and up to 1914, at the heart of the great estates put together in the Sologne region by the old aristocracy or industrial barons. The Sologne combined ideal conditions for hunting with relative proximity to Paris.

Bon Hôtel was built in 1882 by Georges Dupré de Saint-Maur on the site of an ancient castle that commanded the highest point of a great hunting park. Naturally, the owner maintained a pack of stag hounds.

The architects were Clément and Louis Parent, who were tireless builders of mansions in eclectic styles. The models for Bon Hôtel were neighboring Chambord and Chenonceaux. The huge hall, designed to welcome the hunt, is a typical feature of this group of châteaux.

BOUCARD

ABOVE:
Courtyard façade of the right wing, dating from 1560.

OPPOSITE:
External view of the château, which dates from the 15th century.

The place owes its name to a Gascon family that moved to the Berry in the 14th century, and in the 15th century had a château built round a rectangular courtyard. All that survives are the perimeter walls, the corner towers, and the gatehouse barbican. The wing at the back of the courtyard was later demolished to open up the view over the River Sauldre, a tributary of the Cher.

Left and right of the courtyard, the wings illustrate two different moments in the history of the French Renaissance. The left wing was built for Antoine de Boucard, a gentleman at the court of François I from 1520–30, in a style properly described as François I. The right wing is a masterpiece of the Renaissance classicism created very late in François's reign by artists such as Pierre Lescot and Philibert De l'Orme, who were mainly active during the reign of Henri II.

Tympanon of the doorway leading to the staircase of the right wing.

This wing was built in 1560 – the date is inscribed on a chimney shaft – for François de Boucard, son of Antoine and squire to Henri II. On the death of Henri (1559), François de Boucard joined the Reformists and put his arms at the service of their leader Condé, who had strong support in the Berry.

The courtyard façade of this wing is astonishing for the breadth of its piers and the alternation of principal and secondary bays. The doorways on the ground floor were added in the 19th century. The entrance bay is decorated with superposed orders of columns, and leads to a dog-leg staircase. On the upper floor, the wing contains a great hall followed by a large chamber, which have monumental fireplaces, probably contemporary with the main fabric.

Philibert de Montault, placed under house arrest by Louis XIV, lived here from 1671–74, during which brief time he removed the end wing. Quite a number of Loire châteaux lost a wing in the 17th century, changing an enclosed rectangular ground plan to a U-shape. The wing blocking the view to stream or river was generally sacrificed.

One of the fireplaces of the right wing.

BOUMOIS

ABOVE:
Front façade of the house.

RIGHT-HAND PAGE:
Panel of staircase door.

The history of this château is shrouded in mystery. In the 18th century, the Loire in spate carried away the last traces of the first castle, which had been built on an island in the river. It was said to date from the 13th century and to have been razed by the English during the Hundred Years' War.

The choice of the present site, well back from the river and protected by embankments, postdates the 1482 statute concerning the strengthening of embankments. Rebuilding may have taken place at the end of the 15th century, but the decoration of the bays certainly dates from the first decade of the

16th century, as its resemblance to that of Meillant testifies.

The chapel, which was founded in 1530 and consecrated in 1546, is the work of René de Thory, Lord of Boumois, and his wife Anne Asse; this we know from some fine stained glass windows of the 1540s (since destroyed or dispersed) and the dedication to St. Anne, patron saint of the lady founder. However long-lived this couple may have been, we cannot attribute the earliest buildings to them. At the very most, the stair tower door panel is their work, the only surviving piece that is unashamedly Renaissance in style. The lock is a splendid piece of ironwork bearing René's arms.

In the mid-16th century, the château comprised a main house flanked at the rear by two round towers, and at the front by a large pavilion, a stair tower, and a turret containing the chapel annexes. Some low outbuildings enclosed the courtyard, with two (surviving) round towers at the angles. The whole site was surrounded by moats.

The outbuildings were transformed by René Gaultier, a lawyer member of the king's Great Council, who acquired Boumois soon after 1612. In 1628, a flood carried away one wing of the outbuildings. At some point, the moat was moved to create terraces protecting the lower parts of the house, probably the 18th century after René Berthelot, squire of Villeneuve, Commissioner of Audit for Brittany, had acquired Boumois in 1700.

The current owner is removing certain 17th and 18th-century additions and restoring the ground-floor windows to their late 15th early 16th-century form. In addition, an access doorway is being moved from the courtyard to the bottom of the garden.

Gateway to forecourt.

OPPOSITE:
Interior of dovecote.

ABOVE:
Rear and side façades.

BRISSAC

OPPOSITE:
*Entrance façade of the imposing
château.*

ABOVE:
*Left façade. It is noticeable that
the reconstruction of 1614–20,
which was never completed, left
the round towers of the
15th–16th century reconstruction
almost intact. The corner tower
(visible in both photos) contains
the chapel, the presence of*
*which is betrayed by a Gothic
window. Gothic long remained
the style of religious architecture.
The large block adorned with
columns contains the main
staircase. It was intended to be
the centerpiece of the new
façade.*

One château replaces another, making use of the site and re-using the materials. Brissac offers a striking image of this cannabalism. The modern château has not wholly absorbed the old castle; two round towers remain.

The old castle was rebuilt either for the Brézé family in the late 15th century, or for René de Cossé in the early 16th century. De Cossé bought the seigneury of Brissac in 1502, and founded a remarkable family,

descendants of whom still live in the château.

The modern château was built by Charles II de Cossé, first Duke of Brissac, who built it between the years 1614 and 1620. Various architects and master masons were employed. These were local men, of no great reputation: Jacques Corbineau, Leonard Malherbe, René Lemeunier, Michel Huttin, and possibly Julien Dangluze, who also worked for the king at Fontainebleau. The tall

ABOVE:
The kitchen.

OPPOSITE:
Vestibule of great staircase.

pavilion which should have marked the center of the frontispiece is a remarkable example of the classical orders of architecture extended over five stories. A lantern and a statue of Mercury once capped the dome.

Charles's death in 1621 brought building work to a halt. Jeanne Say, widow of the Duke of Brissac who died for his country in 1871, oversaw the restoration of the château and, in 1883, built a delightful theater within the château in 17th-century style.

ABOVE:
The room known as the Louis XIII Room.

OPPOSITE:
The Hunting Room owes its name to six tapestries woven in Flanders in 1570.

THIS PAGE:
Above, the great gallery with the painted ceiling (1625). Below, the great drawing room. At the back is a portrait of the 8th Duke of Brissac.

OPPOSITE:
The theater, constructed in 1883.

CHAMBORD

"What can one say of Chambourg [sic], which, imperfect though it is and only half-finished, excites admiration and rapture in anyone that sees it?" The memorialist Brantôme, writing his *Vie des hommes illustres* at the end of the 16th century, answers the rhetorical question at once: "If the design had been completed as planned, one would count it among the wonders of the world." Dazzling as it is, Chambord as it were conceals a still more astonishing château that might have been.

In the beginning there was a fortress, a forest and a small tributary of the Loire called the Cosson. The fortress was razed to the ground – but the new residence with its heavy square keep, its low perimeter wall and round corner towers was still entirely castellated, like a medieval castle. The forest was enclosed in a wall eight leagues (twenty miles) long, enclosing 13,500 acres. But the diversion of the Loire to make an island of the château, as envisaged by the king, came about only in *Amadis of Gaul*, a novel of chivalry of which François I had ordered the translation in 1543 and in which Chambord appears under the name of the Palace of Firm Isle. In 1519 François I sent in his builders, but work ran into difficulties after the king's defeat at Pavia and subsequent captivity, leading to a break in the works from 1524 to 1526. Construction recommenced in 1526, following a major modification in the plan.

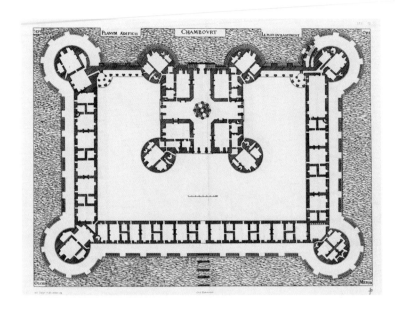

Rear façade and ground plan, taken from the Plus excellents bastiments de France *by Jacques Androuet Du Cerceau (1576).*

Front façade of château.

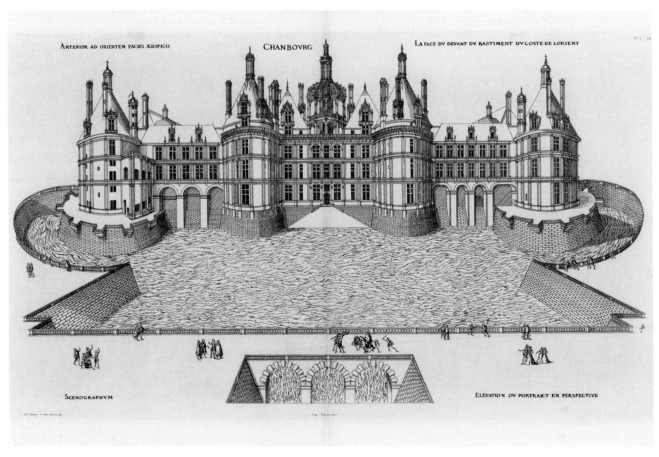

Work on the fabric was finally broken off on the death of Henri II in 1559. Later work from the 17th century to the present day has, in general, left the 16th century work intact.

The records show neither the name of the mastermind behind the 1519 scheme nor what he planned. We can discount the local contractors such as Jacques Sourdeau, Pierre Nepveu (known as Trinqueau) and Jacques Coqueau, who successively became site foreman, as they were certainly illiterate. Apparently Domenico di Cortona, who was one of the Italians brought to France by Charles VIII, was employed at Chambord only as a model maker. One of his models was drawn in the 17th century, when it was clearly in a very poor state. The model shows a more Italianate design than that of the completed building. Nowadays it is agreed that the concept and design should be attributed to Leonardo da Vinci, who had been installed by François at Clos Lucé near Amboise in 1516 and who had just drawn up a plan for a gigantic royal château at Romorantin. In 1519, Leonardo died, just as site work was starting at Chambord. This coincidence no doubt explains some of the problems encountered at the start. Leonardo

ABOVE:
Right courtyard. Note the two round towers of the keep on the left. On the right is the wing in which the François I apartments were created.

OPPOSITE:
Detail of the figure above. With the staircase leading to the François I apartments.

The spiral staircase
with two intertwined flights

One of the oddest and most remarkable things about the house is the steps, made in such a way that one person can go up and another come down without the two meeting each other, although they can see each other. Whereupon Monsieur [Gaston d'Orléans, father of Mademoiselle de Montpensier] immediately took pleasure in playing games with me. He was at the top of the staircase when I arrived. He came down as I went up, and laughed hugely to see me running in expectation of catching him. I was very glad at the pleasure he took, and even more so when I caught up with him.

Mademoiselle de Montpensier (the Grande Mademoiselle), *Mémoires*, 1659

had left little more than an idea, an idea, moreover, so remarkable that the hapless French masons hardly knew what to make of it. The château was to be reduced to a square keep, with round towers at the corners and a single enclosed courtyard. In the middle, the keep would have featured a staircase with four interlaced rises accessing four quarters, resulting from the partition of the interior space by large rooms in the shape of a cross. The division of the façades and arrangement of the apartments was to follow the spiral movement of the staircase and transform the keep into a kind of turbine, one of the machines whose workings Leonardo was studying.

The king's defeat and captivity required a return to reason. An attempt was made to restore the symmetry of the façades. By reducing the staircase to two rises, communication

LEFT-HAND PAGE:
Lantern crowning the central staircase of the keep above the terraces.

ABOVE:
Upper part of the central staircase of the keep. Salamander and F of François I.

Spiral staircase located in the middle of the keep. It consists of two independent ascents, in the same direction and on the same vertical axis.

between the apartments was restored. The king's quarters, which had initially been re-duced to the usual one quarter share, were enlarged by building along the courtyard fronts. The terraces earmarked for watching the pleasures of the hunt were crowned with richly decorated chimneystacks and dormer windows.

The 1519 château was a creation of the mind, a pure Renaissance design. Its arithmetic recurred at the Abbey of Thélème, and it is in his description of this fictional abbey that Rabelais made the first literary reference to Chambord (1532). With its magnificent Gothic roofline, Chambord marked a return to the châteaux of the princes of the lilies. It was a return to the castle of tales and legends, "the palace of [Ariosto's] Alcina and Morgana," as the Venetian ambassador Lippomano put it in 1577.

*Closet forming part of the
François I apartments.
Salamander and F of
François I, fleur-de-lys and
arms with fleur-de-lys.*

An erudite court

Without flattering François I, I can say that I have attended meals with several sovereigns, that I have seen bishops, cardinals and Popes eat, and have never seen a table as erudite as that of the King of France. The readings that are made there, the subjects that are discussed, the conversations that are held, were so instructive that the best-informed person would still find something to learn. There would be profit for the most intelligent of soldiers as much as for the man of letters. I dare say even more, if I am allowed to go into detail; the artist, the gardener and the farmer would have gained new knowledge on hearing the king speak, though he spoke with difficulty and we had to listen keenly to hear him, his illnesses having deprived him of his uvula. A prince with an almost universal genius, if one excepts the Latin tongue, which he did not know.

Hubert Thomas de Liège, diplomat, 1495–1555

Tapestries depicting François I
out hunting, consisting of eight
pieces woven in the first quarter
of the 16th century in the
Parisian district of St. Marcel.
They are based on cartoons by
Laurent Guyot, painter to King
Henri IV. In this reconstitution,
the costumes are indeed those of
François I's time. The two pieces
depict the hunt with falcons.

ABOVE:
Leaving for the hunt.

OPPOSITE:
Releasing the falcons. In the
center, one falcon is already
upon its prey.

OPPOSITE:
One of the eight tapestries
depicting François I out hunting.

ABOVE:
Another series of hunting scenes
involving François I, consisting
of six scenes. This second series
is contemporary with the first. It
was designed by the same artist
and made in the same
workshop, but is distinguishable
from the first by its borders.

RIGHT-HAND PAGE AND THIS
PAGE:

*Two scenes from the second series
of hunting scenes of François I.
The two scenes depict hunting
with falcons, shooting, hunting
with nets, with traps, etc. Oddly,
there is no scene of riding to
hounds, for which the great park
of Chambord is ideally suited.*

Molière's Le Bourgeois Gentilhomme performed at Chambord

The king [Louis XIV], having determined to make a journey to Chambord to enjoy the pleasures of the hunt, wanted to give his court the delight of a ballet as well; and as the memory of the Turks they had just seen in Paris was still very fresh, he thought it would be a good notion to have them appear on stage as well. His Majesty ordered me to get together with Messrs Molière and Lully to compose a play where we could introduce something of the clothes and habits of the Turks. I went therefore to the village of Auteuil, where M. de Molière had a very pretty house. It was there that we worked on *Le Bourgeois Gentilhomme*, who dresses up as a Turk in order to marry the daughter of the Great Lord. As soon as the play was finished, it was shown to the king, who accepted it, and I spent eight hours at Baraillon's, the master tailor's, getting him to make the clothes and turbans in Turkish style. Everything was taken to Chambord, and the play was put on in the month of September. It was a success that satisfied the king and all the court. In fact it was such a success that, although it was repeated several times afterwards, everyone kept asking for it again. People were even wanting to introduce Turkish scenes in the *Ballet de Psyché* that was being prepared for the following carnival. But on consideration, they decided that these two subjects did not really go together.

Chevalier d'Arvieux, 1635–1702, *Mémoires*,
(published in 1735)

CHAMPIGNY-SUR-VEUDE

The château of Champigny was inherited in the 1470s by Louis de Bourbon, born into a cadet branch of the family of the Dukes of Bourbon. In 1498, he founded a college of canons at Champigny, and no doubt started work on the college chapel at the same time.

In 1504, he married his distant cousin Louise de Bourbon-Montpensier. It was apparently in 1508 that he laid the first stone for a new château, and after his death in 1520 the work was continued by his son Louis, first Duke of Montpensier. When the Duke

ABOVE:
The collegiate church. To the right, a doorway leading from the porch to the interior of the collegiate church.

OPPOSITE:
Porch of the collegiate church.

died in 1592 work was certainly very far advanced, if not complete.

Unfortunately, the Montpensiers' château was located very close to that of Richelieu, which the powerful cardinal began to rebuild in the 1630s. The cardinal wanted no competition in the area, and he forced Marie de Montpensier into an exchange that left Champigny in his hands. He then demolished the château, and all that is left of it are the outbuildings, which include the remark-

able Jupiter doorway, a work dating from the second half of the 16th century. Richelieu also wanted to blow up the collegiate church which, like all chapels preserving relics of the Passion, carried the title of Sainte Chapelle. However, the Pope would not hear of it, and it was left to our generation's negligence to accomplish what the cardinal could not – this masterpiece of French architecture, with its exceptional stained glass windows, is falling into disrepair.

The chapel was built in the Gothic style and consecrated in 1545. The windows were commissioned by Cardinal de Givry, uncle of Jacqueline de Givry, whom the Duke of Montpensier married in 1538. The Cardinal may well have had a hand in the construction of the classical porch which fronts the chapel; it is reminiscent of works that the Cardinal commissioned for Langres Cathedral (his

Porch of the collegiate church. The Jupiter pavilion giving access to the service courtyard.

see). The dates 1549 and 1558 are inscribed on the porch; the cardinal died in 1561.

The stained-glass windows illustrate the lives of Christ and St. Louis (Louis XI, from whom the Bourbon-Montpensiers were descended). They show portraits of illustrious members of the family laid to rest in the chapel.

Of the tomb of Henri de Bourbon, erected after his death in 1609 by his daughter Marie, only a kneeling figure remains. This was originally borne on four columns on the screen of the right-hand oratory, which was reserved for the lord of the house, while his wife used the chapel on the left.

The outhouses, the only part of the building to survive apart from the collegiate church.

CHANTELOUP

The 130-foot pagoda is the main surviving relic of the château of Chanteloup. The château was bought in 1761 by Étienne-François de Choiseul, a protégé of Madame de Pompadour, who embarked on a diplomatic career, became a minister, acquired a ducal title in 1757, and between 1758 and 1770 acted more or less in the capacity of prime minister. In 1770 he fell foul of Madame du Barry, who persuaded the king to exile him to Chanteloup.

The pagoda was built between 1773 and 1778 by the architect Louis-Denis Le Camus. It is a monument of gratitude, dedicated by the disgraced minister to the friends who had stuck by him. The Chinese style popularized by the publications of William Chambers and imitated very freely in London's Kew Gardens, is treated even more freely at Chanteloup. There are numerous stories and the roof is slightly curved, but the ornamentation is entirely classical.

The pagoda does not ornament an Anglo-Chinese garden; it is an observatory, placed at the junction of five woodland avenues, allowing observers to watch the hunt.

CHÂTEAUBRIANT

To the right, the old courtyard and Old Castle. To the left, the old outer bailey and the New Château.

The overall layout of this castle – courtyard and bailey – were inherited from a 11th-12th century fortress. Time moved on, and military needs grew less pressing. A new château was constructed in the bailey. The ancient castle buildings around the original courtyard thus became the Old Castle. The old square keep faces both new and old. Under its 14th-century veneer, it is basically 11th or 12th-century work.

The walls of the courtyard and outer bailey and their round towers are quite well preserved, having been rebuilt in the 13th/14th centuries. This is because Châteaubriant,

Wing of the New Château, possibly built by Jean de Laval, whose last commission this would have been (he died in 1543). This wing, built of local schist and brick, nonetheless forms a strong contrast with the main block (visible to the left), which is certainly by him.

astride the borders of Brittany and Anjou, played an important part in the 14th-century Breton war of succession. The two claimants to the ducal title were backed respectively by the kings of France and England. The war was another phase in the long conflict now known as the Hundred Years' War. At the time, the castle was in the hands of Guy XII de Laval, eldest son of a leading Breton family. In 1348, he married the heiress Louise de Châteaubriant and set about reconstructing the original castle. Guy's political vacillations in the conflict are easily explained by the frontier position of the castle. Châteaubriant lay well away from the Loire, to which

later events nevertheless connected it. The Breton issue was still unresolved at the end of the Hundred Years' War. Matters came to a head in 1488, when King Charles VIII, at war with Duke François II of Brittany, laid siege to the castle. The conflict was resolved by marriage. François's daughter and heiress Anne married Charles, and Anne de Bretagne, as Queen of France, ruled her duchy from her Loire Valley residences, both from Nantes, an 'ex-centric' capital for Brittany, and Charles's upper-Loire châteaux of Amboise and Blois. Châteaubriant itself had been reduced to ruins by the royal artillery.

Reconstruction gave Châteaubriant an

Main block of New Château, seen from the portico of the wing.

up in part of the outer bailey. Called the Little Gardens following the creation of the Great Gardens in the mid-16th century, these were themselves indicative of a change in lifestyles, when great importance was attributed to gardens. In numerous châteaux, "little" gardens occupied parts of the outer bailey no longer in use; more extensive gardens were often laid out outside the walls. The Little Gardens at Châteaubriant were enclosed by galleries on three sides, and on the fourth by the new house known as the Green Room House (perhaps because of the presence of the gardens). This house was modernised for Jean de Laval, son and heir of François, who opened up pilastered windows decorated with lozenges and medallions in an Italianate early Renaissance style. They were probably put in soon after Jean de Laval took possession of Châteaubriant in 1503.

Jean de Laval is the main protagonist in the history of the present château. He was a man of exceptional status at the court of François I, since his wife Françoise de Foix was the King's mistress. The payoff was Jean's appointment as governor of Brittany in 1531. At his death in 1543, he had completed the buildings round the outer bailey, now the main courtyard. Jean de Laval's extension of the Green Room shows Châteaubriant moving toward the Blois/Chambord style. Whereas the Green Room was built of the local shale as usual in Brittany, the New House uses the white limestone of the Loire Valley. Even so, transport made it costly, and ashlar was used only around openings, and for pilasters and other ornamentation. The

important place in the history of the ligerian Renaissance. Once again, it was a Laval who set about reconstruction; Guy XIV, who married Françoise de Dinan, heiress to that county, but he left it to his widow († 1500) and their son François († 1503) to refashion the outer bailey with a new lordly residence. This was a very common practice at the time. New buildings could provide the comforts and amenities which were increasingly required in the second half of the 15th century.

The new residence at Châteaubriant was built against the inside of the perimeter wall. The house, dating from the late 15th/early 16th century, looks out onto gardens opened

rubble-stone walls were discreetly hidden under a coat of plaster. Limestone was not the only Ligerian trimming. The staircase was dogleg (not spiral), there were casement windows, dormers, pilasters, and medallions. The style is more advanced than that of Azay-le-Rideau or Blois. The flights of the staircase are roofed with a Renaissance barrel vault, not Gothic rib vaulting. The pilasters superpose the classical orders — more or less as required by the architectural treatises. Does the inscribed date 1587 indicate when the New House was finished? It does not tell us when work started, or how advanced it was for its time. It is hard to accept, for example, that the return wing, which features a portico on the ground floor and a gallery upstairs, and terminates in an open pavilion containing a staircase, is still the work of Jean de Laval. The differences between it and the New Château are too great. Apertures, pilasters and moldings are once again built of Breton schist, with brick infilling between. The Tuscan columns of the portico and the semi-circular arches and pediments of the dormers belong to the pure classicism of the treatises. We do not know whether it was completed or even begun before Jean de Laval's death. One famous anecdote suggests an early date. The *Contes d'Eutrapel* recount how a Breton mason, summoned to exercise his skills at Châteaubriant, was taken aback to find erudite architects "talking of frontispieces, pedestals, obelisks, columns, capitals, friezes, plinths such as he'd never heard of."

Staircase of the main block.

CHÂTEAUDUN

Nicole Duval built the finest parts of this château during the third quarter of the 15th century for Jean d'Orléans.

Nicole – a male and female name at the time – came from Rouen, where he was the city's master of works but he is not otherwise known. Jean, the Bastard of Orléans, who became famous during his campaigns against the English at the side of Joan of Arc, was one of the most important and cultured of the great lords surrounding the king. The chronicler Jean Chartier calls him "one of the finest speakers of the French language [there has] ever [been]." Son of Duke Louis I of Orléans and therefore nephew of King Charles VI, he was given the county of Dunois, with its capital of Châteaudun, by his half-brother Charles d'Orléans, the poet and Count of Blois.

The building, which was begun in 1451, was aimed solely at proclaiming the handsome Dunois's rank as a prince of the blood. The work that can be attributed to him at Châteaudun was almost finished when he was legitimized in 1465. Thereafter he was able to hand down his coat of arms to his descendants of the branch of Valois-Longueville without the bend sinister of bastardy. (Dunois was also granted the county of Longueville by the king.)

It is significant that the keep of the Counts of Dunois was preserved. The tower is attributed to Thibaud V, Count of Blois, and if so would be virtually contemporary with the keep at the Louvre. Built at the end of the 12th century, the latter exemplified a type of keep consisting of a large cylindrical tower which had first appeared early in the century.

The keep at Châteaudun is one of the more imposing examples, being 55 feet in diameter and 100 feet high. A single door 32 feet from the ground leads to the upper hall. From there, a stairway goes down into the lower hall through a hole pierced in the crown of the vault.

Reconstruction of the chapel began in 1451. The chapel has more than one floor, a common occurrence in princely residences; but here the tradition was inverted, and the princely family used the lower chapel while the servants were relegated to the upper. In 1456, Dunois obtained from the king a piece of the True Cross taken from the relic acquired by Louis IX, which the saintly king had taken care to preserve at the Sainte-Chapelle,

LEFT-HAND PAGE:
External façade of the Longueville wing (left) and end of the Dunois wing (right).

ABOVE:
Left: the keep and the chapel masking the Dunois wing. Right: the courtyard façade of the Longueville wing.

The monumental spiral staircases of the 15th and 16th centuries were constructed as separate towers. The novelty here is that the staircase is contained within the house, and does not project from the façade. To create a circular stairwell behind flat walls, the architect was obliged to leave empty space between the two.

the two-storied chapel of the palace of the Cité in Paris. The chapel at Châteaudun was then promoted to the rank of *sainte chapelle*, a title given only to churches that preserved a relic of the Passion. They are all, in fact, princely foundations. Here again Dunois's motivation is clear. The chapel initially consisted only of the present choir. In 1461, a nave was added, bringing it in contact with the so-called Dunois wing, construction of

which was begun at the same time. It was completed in 1464. Around 1494, Agnès de Savoie, widowed by the death in 1491 of François de Longueville, the son and heir of Dunois, added two oratories, a statue of Ste. Agnès and a great wall painting of the Last Judgment.

The Dunois wing culminates in a large staircase. Whatever the date of its construction (1464?), this spiral staircase is an impor-

tant milestone in the history of staircases. Like the great spiral staircase of the Louvre, a landmark monument of the Valois dynasty constructed for Charles V in the 1360s, the staircase at Châteaudun is open and its façade decorated with statues. The statues in the Louvre constituted a kind of Valois family tree. Probably Dunois took this opportunity to emphasize his lineage. The avant-garde aspects of this staircase are firstly that it is wholly integrated, and secondly, that its landings form loggias. The decoration in the Flamboyant style was finished by Agnès de

Savoie († 1508), whose arms feature on several keystones. The wing which extends beyond the Dunois staircase, called the Longueville wing, was begun only after the death of Dunois in 1468 and not completed until 1518. The tour de force here is another open spiral staircase from 1510, taking up where the Dunois staircase left off, this time with Renaissance decoration. It was probably commissioned by François II, son of Agnès de Savoie and first Duc de Longueville, and executed by the master masons Jean Barreau, Olivier Chollet and Pierre Gadier.

CHAUMONT

The two interlaced 'C's of Charles II d'Amboise, one of the builders of the château, are visible in several places. They represent him and his wife Catherine de Chauvigny. Also evident are a burning mount (chaud mont), a punning emblem, and the arms of Cardinal Georges d'Amboise. The Cardinal supervised the construction in the absence of his nephew Charles, who was the king's lieutenant general in the Milanese.

The reconstruction of the château between 1466 and 1510 was the work of the Amboise family, who had owned Chaumont since the 12th century. The château was originally enclosed within four wings round a court that was almost square. The angles were cardinal at the four points, as in most French châteaux of the period. Like many Loire châteaux, Chaumont was opened out in the 18th century by the demolition of a wing, in this case the northeast wing. The northeast and northwest wings and associated towers, constituting half the château, were built for Pierre d'Amboise and his son Charles I († 1481). The construction of the second half of the quadrilateral, with the entrance between twin towers and the great staircase, was begun on the orders of Charles II, son of Charles I, and ceased at his death in 1510. Charles II was one of the most eminent members of his family – in 1501 he was made governor of the Milanese by Louis XII, a position he held until his death. As his appointment kept him far from Chaumont, it is thought that the works were supervised by his uncle, Cardinal Georges d'Amboise, Archbishop of Rouen. The cardinal was King Louis XII's all-powerful minister and one of the great prelates of the Renaissance; he built the château of Gaillon, first masterpiece of the early French Renaissance. It is therefore surprising to note the very traditional character of Chaumont, which displays few

ABOVE:
General view of the château, with the two entrance towers in the foreground.

LEFT:
17th-century stained glass windows depicting (left) the construction of the Temple at Jerusalem by Solomon, and (right) King Solomon meeting the Queen of Sheba.

Catherine de' Medici at Chaumont

"The queen mother Catherine de' Medici, being desirous to know if all her children would rise to the Rank, a magician at the château of Chaumont showed her (...), around a circle he had prepared, all the kings of France there had been and would be, who made as many turns around the circle as they had reigned and should reign in years; and as Henry the Third had made fifteen turns, behold the late king (Henri IV), who entered the course strong and fit, who made twenty turns and, wanting to complete the twenty-first, disappeared. After him came a little prince eight or nine years old, who made thirty-seven or thirty-eight turns; and after that every thing made itself invisible, because the late queen mother did not want to see any more."

Nicolas Pasquier, *Lettres*, 1623

OPPOSITE:
The access to the entrance courtyard, which is defended externally by two towers (see preceding pages).

ABOVE:
Fireplace with the arms of Cardinal Georges d'Amboise.

Most of the interior features (notably the vault of the staircase) were remodeled or added in the 19th century.

Italianate features; but even at Gaillon the Italian style did not appear before 1508. In 1560, the Queen Mother, Catherine de' Medici, bought Chaumont, apparently intending to exchange it for Diane de Poitier's Chenonceaux. (The widow – Henri II died in 1559 – was magnanimous toward the mistress). Although Catherine's stay there was very short, Chaumont is thought to be the site of the royal astrologer's prediction; he informed her of the rapid succession of her sons on the throne, the sudden end of the Valois line and the arrival of the Bourbons in the person of Henri IV.

In the 19th century, Chaumont underwent partial remodeling in the Renaissance style by Jules de la Morandière, working for Viscount Walsh, who acquired the château in 1847. Even more drastic changes followed in 1878 at the hands of Paul-Ernest Simon, a prolific architect of pastiche châteaux, who was working for Prince Amédée de Broglie.

CHENONCEAUX

Chenonceaux is surely one of the most remarkable and yet most representative of Loire châteaux. After crossing the courtyard with its offices and outhouses, the visitor encounters a circular tower standing by itself, then a centrally planned château, and finally a galleried bridge built on two stories. The sequence is chronological. The tower is what remains of the château built in 1432 by Jean II Marques, a faithful follower of King Charles VII. The Marques family had been holders of the fief of Chenonceaux since the 13th century. The Marques Tower was preserved by Thomas Bohier, who took possession of Chenonceaux in 1513 and built the centrally planned château. The preservation of the medieval keep or of a tower described as such was current practice; but at Chenonceaux the tower is placed right by the entrance, in unwonted isolation.

Thomas Bohier, Receiver-General for Normandy, married Catherine Briçonnet, daughter of a Touraine family of financiers. He died in 1524, three years before the trial of Jacques de Beaune-Semblançay, who was Receiver-General of finances – the equivalent of a modern Minister of Finance. He brought the Bohiers down with him in his fall. Thomas Bohier's château is a kind of bulky house on a square ground plan flanked by turrets. It was constructed, not on the foundations of the old château (as custom required), but on those of a mill built across

View from upstream. On the extreme right is the Marques Tower, a survival from the castle built in 1432 for Jean de Marques II. On the right, the château built in the waters of the Cher for Thomas Bohier in the 1510s. On the left, the bridge with two floors of galleries, begun by Philibert De l'Orme for Diane de Poitiers and completed by Jean Bullant for Catherine de' Medici.

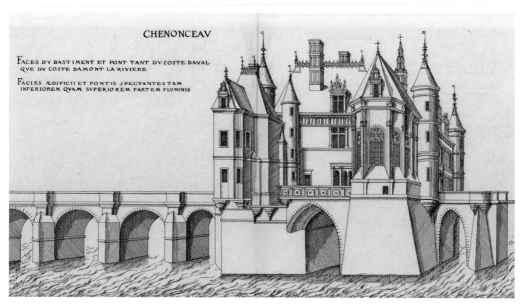

CHENONCEAV

FACES DV BASTIMENT ET PONT TANT DV COSTE DAVAL
QVE DV COSTE DAMONT LA RIVIERE

FACIES ÆDIFICII ET PONTIS SPECTANTES TAM
INFERIOREM QVAM SVPERIOREM PARTEM FLVMINIS

CHENONCEAV

FACES DV BASTIMENT ET PONT TANT DV COSTE
DAVAL QVE DV COSTE DAMONT LA RIVIERE

FACIES ÆDIFICII ET PONTIS SPECTANTES TAM
INFERIOREM QVAM SVPERIOREM PARTEM FLVMINIS

THIS PAGE:
*Views of Bohier's château before
the construction of the galleries,
taken from* Les plus excellents
bastiments de France *by
Jacques Androuet Du Cerceau
(1579). Above, view from
upstream. Below, view from
downstream.*

RIGHT-HAND PAGE:
*The galleried bridge spanning
the Cher.*

ABOVE:
The great central passage which passes right through Bohier's château and leading to the entrance on the bridge.

RIGHT-HAND PAGE:
The room known as Diane de Poitiers's Room, with its 19th-century fireplace.

the Cher. The *dans-œuvre* staircase has straight flights and is situated in the middle of the corridor. The fabric of the château and overall style of its decoration are still Gothic in spirit, but the ground plan and staircase are innovations. This is hardly surprising; Bohier went on the Italian expeditions led by Charles VIII, Louis XII and François I. The long corridor leading to the light and the water is perhaps an echo of Venice. In 1535, the Bohiers sold Chenonceaux to François I to pay their debts. Henri II presented it to his favorite Diane de Poitiers. When Henri died, the queen took revenge by forcing Diane to take Chaumont in exchange. The two rivals between them created the galleried bridge. In 1556, Diane commissioned Philibert De l'Orme to design a bridge with a low gallery. Only the bridge was built, slightly off axis in relation to the corridor to connect with the window, which was integral to the design of the Bohier château.

Work ceased in 1559 on Henri II's death. Catherine's plan for two large superposed galleries (1570–76) profoundly changed the scale of the château. Even this is no more than a tiny part of an immense scheme typical of the architectural mania of the Wars of Religion. The offices at the entrance were to be the first part of a trapezoidal forecourt. The architect is unknown: Denis Courtin, the obscure clerk of works at the château, or Jean Bullant, Queen Catherine's architect?

the waters of the Cher. If we except the chapel and library, which project from one façade, the ground plan is central and divided into modules. Each unit is equal to the width of the corridor crossing the entire château down the middle, leading from the entrance to a window which formerly opened onto

ABOVE:
Room of Louise of Lorraine,
wife of King Henri III. The
funereal decor is a recreation,
and shows the room as
decorated for the royal widow
after her husband's
assassination.

LEFT-HAND PAGE:
The room known as the
Catherine de' Medici Room.
The decoration dates from the
19th century.

Rousseau at Chenonceaux

"In 1747, we went to spend the autumn in Touraine, at the château of Chenonceaux, a royal house on the Cher built by Henri the Second for Diane de Poitiers, whose initials can still be seen, and which is now owned by Monsieur Dupin, the Farmer General [of taxes]. We had a very enjoyable time in this lovely place. The food was excellent, and I became as plump as a monk. There was a lot of music-making. I composed several trios for voice there, full of excellent harmony, which I will come back to in my postscript, if I ever write one. We acted comedies. I wrote a three-act one in a fortnight called *The Reckless Engagement*, which will be found among my papers and whose only merit is great jollity. I also wrote some other little pieces there, among other things a verse play called *Sylvia's Avenue*, which is the name of an avenue in the park that borders the Cher. And all this was done without interrupting my work on chemistry and what I was doing with Mme Dupin."

Jean-Jacques Rousseau, *Confessions*, 1770

CHEVERNY

The château of Cheverny was built in the 1620s and 1630s (probably from 1625) for Henri Hurault, *lieutenant général* to the administration of Orléans, governor and bailiff of Blois († 1648), by Jacques Bougier, a master mason from the Blois area († 1632), who may simply have been the builder.

An important alteration, dating from the 18th century, was the demolition of the wings and the fence that closed the courtyard. At the same time, banded rustication was applied to the courtyard façade, which perhaps conceals a mixed bond like that of the rear façade (dressed stone and rubble covered with plaster, probably once painted as sham brickwork). While these alterations were unknown, it was thought that Cheverny was a very early example of a château without wings and with continuous rustication, whereas this château illustrates – to perfection – a fashion already on its way out, that of houses consisting of individual pavilions. Differentiating the pavilions by function was once a sign of modernity: the central pavilion is entirely filled by the staircase; the broad pavilions at the side, of double depth, contain the apartments, while the narrower intermediate pavilions contain rooms opening onto both façades. The 1640s interior decoration, consisting of paneling, painted ceilings, and fireplaces, and paintings by Jean Monnier, is among the finest of its kind.

This 17th-century façade originally faced onto a courtyard. The wings and enclosure were removed in the 18th century.

LEFT-HAND PAGE:
Principal staircase. It bears the date 1634. It belongs to a type that was widespread in France throughout the 16th century: a dogleg staircase in which straight flights are separated only by a wall, which in this case is pierced with arcades. A new type, in which the stairs turn round a central void, made its appearance in the 1640s.

ABOVE:
The great drawing room is a recreation of the 19th century. The paneling dates from this century. The portraits are from various sources. The grisaille love scenes in the lower part are the only remnant of the early 17th-century decor.

**The gods of antiquity
in the "Metamorphoses" of Ovid and the decoration at Cheverny**

Your writings, Ovid, no longer pass for fables.
The gods of your pretence are deities in flesh,
And here is where they pass their time,
Constantly preoccupied with the very things
That your muse depicts in your metamorphoses
And art presents to us as living gods.

We also see the selfsame bed whereon lay goddesses
When the gods came down for their caresses,
We see whence Pasiphae is born
The bed where Jupiter appeared as rain
Still ablaze with gold, a hand that sweeps it up
Each time he thither came to sport with Danaë.

Anonymous 17th-century poem about Cheverny

The King's Chamber (a name traditionally given to the best room in the house) is adorned with remarkable paintings by Jean Monnier from the 1640s. The main subject is the story of Perseus, the hero of antiquity. On the fireplace, Perseus turns his enemies to stone by showing them the head of Medusa, which he has just cut off. The lower panels depict the love of Theagenes and Charicles, from a 16th-century novel. The scene over the door was perhaps removed as being too risqué.

The state of the château of Cheverny in 1764 according to Durfort, its new owner

Cheverny had been abandoned to a steward five years earlier ... The forecourt, whose walls were flush with the ground, was high with wheat up to the steps of the staircase. The immense paving stones were buried under soil and seeded. The casement windows of the château were entirely glazed in diamond panes ...

The great château, made up of five pavilions, roofed with two domes, had in all only five habitable rooms between them. The rest were corridors in immense storehouses. Everything was in a deplorable state ...

I wanted to make Cheverny as habitable and pleasant as possible. Monsieur de Cypierre brought me his architect, who assured me that he would do everything for 30,000 livres, while he told others it would cost 100,000 écus ... I began by completing the entrance bridge, clearing the main courtyard and uncovering the paving; I got rid of the diamond-paned casements entirely. The dovecote still existed in my time, and I was the one who had it demolished. The cellars of the château are still partly extant and the moats, once full of water, are still visible.

The improvements that I made at Cheverny made it more and more habitable every day. I arranged to do a pavilion every winter; there were five of them, so it would take five years. I made contracts, and they were adhered to, so that I took possession each time I returned and all I had to do was furnish ...

One winter was dedicated to buying marble fireplaces. I needed twenty-seven ... I visited ... all the monumental masons in Paris and I only bought reject fireplaces ... Another year I went shopping for sixty English brass locks, so that after twelve years I had made this château one of the most habitable in the province ."

During the Revolution, Durfort took steps to save the decoration of the château from being vandalized:

"In decorating the exterior of the château, I had had the main drive lined with large upright stones so that no-one would walk on the lawns, and had run a chain strung from stone to stone. I had the stones buried – so deep that I still have them. I also had a bell buried, an antique monument taken from a convent by the Huraults and used to summon people to meals. In the chapel of the château was a white marble Virgin four foot high. I had it secretly buried in the park ...

Each pier of the château had Greek marble busts between the windows which I knew were Roman emperors; I told them they were sans-culottes Greek philosophers – and in this way kept them."

J N Durfort, *Mémoires sur les règnes de Louis XV et de Louis XVI et sur la Révolution*, posthumous edition, 1886

Hunting Museum. There is still staghunting at Cheverny.

CHINON

Clock Tower, dating from the late 14th century. The tower also serves as a gateway to the Middle Castle.

Chinon is difficult to miss, perched as it is atop a rocky spur overlooking the River Vienne, about six miles from where the tributary runs into the Loire. The town covers the space between the river and the spur, which has been occupied since prehistoric times. Traces of a Roman castrum have been discovered there. The site was long the subject of a dispute between the powerful rival houses of Blois and Anjou. A fragment of the enclosure wall built in the second half of the 10th century by the Count of Blois, Thibaud le Tricheur still stands; and there are significant

remains of the post-1160 building work commissioned by Henry II Plantagenet, scion of the House of Anjou, King of England. Chinon was at the center of his French domains. Thereafter, the Plantagenets and the Capetians fought for possession of Chinon. In 1205, the capture of the castle by Philippe Auguste enabled him to restore Touraine to France.

From east to west of the spur, three areas are distinguishable, separated by moats. Fort Saint-Georges, created *ex nihilo* by King Henry II, increased the castle's dominance. The central area is called the Château du Milieu (Middle Castle). Access to it is via the clock tower, a gatehouse that guards the bridge crossing the first moat. In this area was Henry II's keep, which was destroyed in the siege of 1205. Traces still remain of the main residence, with the great hall built for Charles VII. In 1429, Charles received Joan of Arc in this building, when she sought out the Dauphin to take him to Rheims and be crowned king of France. Chinon was then the capital of the legitimate heir to the king of France, while the title had been carried off to Paris by the king of England.

The moat that isolates the Coudray fortress, at the extreme western end of the spur, was excavated only after the siege of 1205. This round keep is typical of those built by Philippe Auguste's engineers; the best-known was that of the Louvre.

Ruin progressively took hold of the castle from the 17th century on, more as the result

of neglect than systematic destruction. A remedy came only in 1854, when the building was classified as a historic monument, after pressure from the writer Prosper Mérimée.

The Chinon keep earned notoriety as the place where the Templars were imprisoned after Philippe IV (Philip the Fair), coveting their enormous wealth, suppressed the order in 1307.

The Clock Tower (extreme right). At the focal point, the royal residence. The Mill Tower (extreme left), forms part of the Coudray Fort.

Ruins of the royal house, the great hall of which was built in the 1420s by Charles VII. It was here that he received Joan of Arc.

Charles VIII and Joan of Arc

"I myself was present in the town and at the castle of Chinon [on 9th March 1429], and I saw her appear before the royal majesty with great humility and simplicity, that poor little shepherd maid."

Raoul de Gaucourt, Governor of Orléans, *Mémoires*

"Thus, having come before the king, Joan made the curtseys and bows customarily made to the king like someone reared at court, and having made her salutations, said, addressing the king: 'God grant you long life, noble Dauphin!' even though she did not know him and had never seen him; and there were several lords, grandly clothed and more opulently so than the king. He therefore replied to the said Joan, 'But I am not the King, Joan'. And pointing to one of his lords, said, 'That's the king.' At which she replied: 'In the name of God, noble prince, you are he and none other.'"

John Chartier, *Chronique de Charles VII*

Joan told [the king in private conversation] a certain secret that no-one knew or could know except God. That is why he had great confidence in her. I heard all that from the lips of Joan, because I myself was not present."

Brother John Pasquerel, Joan's confessor

Moat separating the Middle Castle (right) from the Coudray Fort (left). The Coudray Tower or keep was constructed in the early 13th century by Philippe Auguste.

FOUGÈRES-SUR-BIÈVRE

ABOVE:
Courtyard, with entrance (center).

BELOW:
Doorway of house.

Fougères is arranged round a square court-yard, with a forecourt in front of it, and a garden behind. Originally it was surrounded by water-filled moats. Entrance is through a curtain wall defended by clusters of round towers and a heavy, square building wrongly called a keep. The wing at the back of the court and the right-hand wing make up the residential quarters. The left wing is only a gallery that leads to the chapel.

Building work lasted from the last decades of the 15th century to the first decades of the 16th century. The oldest part is the house. The doorway to it is adorned with angels carrying escutcheons, now blank, but formerly bearing the arms of the Refuge family. The family acquired possession of Fougères by marriage in 1438, but the buildings are attributed to Pierre de Refuge, who succeeded his father in 1475. Pierre carved out a fine career as Minister of Finance for several provinces under Charles VII and Louis XI, and obtained royal permission to "re-establish the building at Fougères as a castle". He died in 1497.

The entrance wing with its round towers and house may be his work, but it is more probably that of his grandson and successor in 1497, Jean de Villebresmes, chamberlain of the Duke of Alençon and subsequently governor of Rodez (1516). It was he who had the gallery-wing and chapel built. Apart from a few Italianizing features discreetly added to

Entrance wing.

the main house when the gallery was being constructed, the château is typical of those in the Loire during the second half of the 15th century. Access to the various parts is via open galleries and spiral stairtowers or through the courtyard, which is reached directly from the principal room of the lower residential floor. The decoration is restrained and austere, in total contrast with both the early Flamboyant style and the Italianate motifs of the Renaissance.

GIEN

One of the emblems on the façade.

Louis XI gave Gien to his daughter Anne de France, wife of Pierre III de Bourbon, the Lord of Beaujeu. Anne was regent during the minority of her brother Charles VIII and during his Italian expedition in 1496. She had the château built at the very end of the 15th century on the site of an earlier one.

Neither Anne's château at Gien nor Charles' at Amboise display any of the influences brought back to France with the royal expedition. This is the more suprising in that the

first expedition had an immediate effect on the construction of the Bourbon château at Moulins, another of Anne de Beaujeu's works.

Gien is one of the best examples in the Loire Valley of the French Renaissance style that preceded Italianism. The design and ground plan were conceived mainly in terms of comfort and convenience rather than defense, decoration being obtained by the patterned brickwork rather than ornamenta-

tion. Colored and glazed bricks arranged into various motifs were in vogue, but at Gien the motifs themselves are very unusual, and not often found elsewhere. Notable among them are the star of Solomon and a rectangle incorporating the golden section, which might refer to Masonic traditions. What are we to make of these emblems on the house of a daughter of France?

Courtyard façades.

GOULAINE

The main house with its two stair towers was built for Christophe II, Gentleman of the Bedchamber first to Louis XII, and later to François I, and Lord of Goulaine from 1492 to 1533. The fortified perimeter wall, much of which has survived, was built in 1585–95 during the Wars of the League. Gabriel de Goulaine, who was *lieutenant général* of the Union in Anjou and Poitou, was among the last Leaguers to rally to the cause of Henri IV. Henri made him a marquis, to ensure the loyalty of this powerful family, though the title was only ratified by the Breton Parliament in 1632.

Ratification was considered a good enough reason to carry out important works on the château at that date, including the construction of the chapel wing as a right-hand return wing to the main house; the construction of the stable as a left-hand return wing; and interior decoration with great fireplaces, paneling, and paintings on both paneling and ceiling.

Looking at the astonishing symmetry of the composition facing the court, we might be tempted to imagine the main house in its original Flamboyant style, scarcely influenced by the approaching Renaissance; it dates from the late 15th and early 16th century. The staircase towers were designed to be at the corners so we can be sure that the wings were intended from the outset, and perhaps even erected, where the 17th century wings (chapel and stables) were later built. In the piano nobile, if we eliminate internal partition walls without chimneys, we find that each staircase provided access to a large room illuminated by two casements on both the courtyard side and the rear, plus a smaller room lit only from the rear. In the right wing, this arrangement still prevails.

In the 15th century, internal circulation was not well understood, and several staircase towers were needed, though one of these was generally considered the main staircase. The equality of division (or near equality, as the right-hand tower is slightly larger) and the symmetry (particularly surprising in the decoration of the towers, bearing in mind the fact that the right-hand tower has lost one of its dormers) must have had some significance, which only history, genealogy or blazonry can reveal. The tradition of twin main buildings went back a long way, and continued to Versailles. We do not need to go far to find several examples of a king-queen division in the royal châteaux of the Loire. The answer lies in the unidentified monogram of the left-hand tower, an exact counterpart of the three As, emblem of the Goulaines, on the right-hand tower. This emblem, topped by two crowns, reads "A cettuy ci et a cettuy la accorday les couronnes" and recalls the mediation of Matthew of Goulaine in restoring peace between the Kings of France and England in 1160 and 1184, which resulted in the Goulaines being allowed to carry a coat of arms party per pale of France and England. Deciphering the monogram should lead to the descendants of the wife of Christophe II.

As for the château itself, it is divided like an escutcheon, indicating its double adherence to Upper Brittany and the Loire Valley: local shale at the rear, Saumur limestone at the front.

LE GRAND-PRESSIGNY

Le Grand-Pressigny is famous for its prehistoric stone-dressing workshops, which give some indication of how long the site has been occupied. The first written record of the name dates from the 6th century. The keep and its chemise were built at the end of the 12th century by Guillaume I de Pressigny. The site's importance was political: it lay at the point where the king of France's holdings bordered the king of England's. In recognition of its crucial position, in 1204 Philippe Auguste raised Guillaume to the rank of knight-banneret. The keep originally featured wooden hoards, but in the early 15th century these were replaced by stone machicolations. Unfortunately, in 1988 torrential rain brought down two of the keep's four walls. The curtain wall with its round towers, which encloses the courtyard and outer bailey, is a patchwork of building and rebuilding from the 14th–16th centuries.

The house stands between courtyard and outer bailey, in the heart of the castle precinct. A 16th-century work, it is normally attributed in its entirety to Honorat de Savoie, who inherited Pressigny on the death of his father René in 1545, the latter having acquired it in 1523. René, who was known as the Grand bâtard de Savoie, was half-brother to Louise de Savoie, the mother of François I. Honorat's family name was Savoie-Villars, since he had also inherited the county and then the marquisate of Villars. He was an important figure at the French royal court through five reigns, from François I to Henri III. His work on the house at Pressigny must date from around 1560, though this date can only apply to certain parts, including the Vironne Tower, the stair tower which today stands curiously isolated; the kiosk covering a well at the foot of the keep; and possibly the wing that separates the courtyard from the outer bailey and which features a portico on the ground floor and a gallery on the upper floor. But the façades of this wing are certainly several decades older. They may even have been erected in the time of René, before 1525. If so, Honorat is responsible only for the internal arrangements.

LE GUÉ-PÉAN

The château of Le Gué-Péan consists of three wings around a rectangular court, the fourth side being enclosed by a wall containing the entrance gateway. The gateway is flanked by two round towers, while four other round towers mark the outside corners. These towers (more especially the front pair) are probably remnants of a medieval castle.

The château was progressively modernized in the course of the 16th and first half of the 17th centuries. The modernization was begun by Nicolas Alamand, a financier from Angers who grew rich by embezzling. Alamand died in 1527, just at the moment when Financial Secretary Jacques de Beaune, who had become involved in his schemes, was arrested and executed. Nicolas' son François Alamand was nonetheless appointed Controller General of salt tax in 1535, and became deputy president of the Audit Office in 1550. Work on rebuilding probably stopped in 1527, and resumed after François Alamand had obtained the promotion of the lordship of Le Gué-Péan to a castellany in 1543. The oldest features of the decoration suggest a 1540s date, and were therefore almost certainly commissioned by François, who died in 1555.

However, his successors were also active.

The bridge (left) gives access to the entrance inserted in the 16th or 17th century by demolishing an enclosing wall.

Courtyard façade of left wing, with a corner tower with imperial roof.

The upper parts of the front tower with its imperial-style roof bears the date 1581. The only contract to have survived was signed in 1584 with the masons of Blois, who agreed to implement a design by Jehan du Bourg, master mason of Orléans. The works were commissioned by Jean Alamand, son of François. His intention was undoubtedly to put similar imperial-style roofs on all the towers.

The monumental fireplaces in mid-17th century style bear the monogram FACP, which could be that of François II, son of Jean,

Mid-17th-century fireplace.

Lord of Le Gué-Péan from 1600 to 1621, and his wife Charlotte de Prie, or more probably that of Charlotte Alamand, who inherited the château in 1649, and her husband François de Picques, the king's majordomo. The rebuilding of the courtyard façades seems likely to be their work too.

These few isolated facts about the château do not amount to a full history and a number of features remain unexplained. These could be accounted for if we imagine a 90° reorientation of the buildings. In that case, the present entrance would have been created in the 16th or 17th century by sacrificing either a whole block of the building or possibly a forecourt. In the Middle Ages, the entrance would have been in the part of the right wing transformed in the 17th century into a portico bearing a terrace.

L'ISLE SAVARY

In 1464, Guillaume de Varye paid the not inconsiderable sum of 400,000 crowns for a castle which had belonged to the Savary family during the Middle Ages and still bears their name. Varye was a rich cloth merchant from Bourges and a colleague of Jacques Cœur, Charles VII's famous treasurer. In 1448, the king appointed Varye as his groom of the bedchamber. Later he awarded him the bailiwick of Touraine, and finally granted him letters patent of nobility. The trial and conviction of Jacques Cœur was a setback for Varye, but the advent of Louis XI (1461) reestablished his credit at the court. The book of hours called *Vie à mon désir*, the illuminations of which are attributed to Jean Fouquet, was commissioned by Varye.

The château consists of three wings framing a courtyard, leaving the fourth side open. The courtyard was originally closed on this side as well, by a wall which was later removed, perhaps in the 18th century. A bridge was then constructed to complete the new entrance. Previously, access had been via the left wing, which still bears the toothing of the doorways and drawbridges. Two spiral staircases in the courtyard were torn down at the same time, to be replaced by a staircase with straight flights. This removed one of the characteristic features of 15th-century aristocractic architecture. The château is flanked at the four corners by square towers beneath tall pavilion roofs. Three of these towers are virtually the same. The fourth is much bigger and has the appearance of a keep, and there is every reason to suppose that Varye was in fact happy to retain and convert the medieval keep. The history of French châteaux provides many examples of these witnesses to seignorial power being preserved, even at the expense of the general arrangement. Thanks to these square (rather than round) towers and the way the wings composed of similar pavilion blocks meet at right angles, L'Isle Savary displays a precocious modernity. But the keep and the left wing with the original entrance are set askew. The question is whether Varye lacked the money to complete his program of regularization or whether he was deliberately contrasting tradition and modernity. However surprising it may seem,

the second hypothesis is not unlikely. The contrast occurs in several châteaux, notably at Verdelles (q.v.).

Machicolation of one of the towers.

JUSSY-CHAMPAGNE

Jussy-Champagne is set in the Berry countryside, where fields of wheat stretch away toward the distant horizon; its only connection with the Loire valley is the Cher, which flows into the Loire. Construction was begun in 1584 by François de Gamaches, leader of the Berry royalists during the Wars of Religion, and completed by his grandson, Claude de Gamaches, who was one of the many inhabitants of Berry committed to la Fronde. The castle twice bore the brunt of civil wars which tore families apart; here the grandfather was a royalist caught between the Sainte-Ligue and the Protestants, while the grandson favoured insurrection. By

contrast, the castle's unity was maintained despite the fifty year gap in construction work. The fashion for mixing brick and stone ensured this. It is thought to have originated in the Loire Valley during the second half of the 15th century, and spread first to Paris, then to France as a whole. During the period 1580–1640, it was the prevailing fashion.

The interior layout of the main house is typical of a pattern, which, widespread in the 16th century, slowly died out in the first half of the 18th. The servants' quarters were in the basement, the dogleg staircase occupied the full width of the house, and there was a single large ground-floor room on either side

of it. Françoise de Gamaches built the left-hand half of the house with the central projection that hides the staircase, the short return wing, and a large pavilion at the rear corner on the garden side.

The state of the château at the end of the 19th century is known to us through an engraving by Chastillon. Claude completed the house itself, built a second wing, but postponed the construction of a matching pavilion. It was never built. But Claude commissioned from Jean Lejuge, an architect from Bourges, a remarkable extension of the buildings that enclose the courtyard. On either side, there is a low galleried wing, at

the end of which stands a large pavilion flanked by a smaller one which contains the staircase. The jumble of buildings that results is very picturesque; there is a great variety of coverings, while the facades are rusticated and have projecting dormers. These are the traditional accompaniment to the poly-chrome bond of the Louis XIII style – which is incorrectly so called, since, though it ended during his reign, it was born some fifty years earlier in the court of the last of the Valois dynasty.

Main house. The left part is from the 16th century, the right from the 17th century.

LANGEAIS

Langeais is in Touraine but close to Anjou. All that is left for the visitor to see today is a ruined keep and an unfinished main house. The keep was probably constructed at the end of the 10th century by Foulques Nerra, the powerful Count of Anjou, while the house was built in the second half of the 15th century for King Louis XI. Sited at the top of the spur which dominates the confluence of the Loire and the Roumer, the keep is among the best preserved Romanesque *donjons* in the Valley. The main house stands well below it, clearly showing that it was not built for warfare, despite its forbidding aspect.

The spartan decoration was determined by the thrift, not to say avarice, of the King himself. The rebarbative forms, many of them defensive features (drawbridge and rampart walk), were the precautions of a timid monarch who had little to fear. Touraine belonged to him; Anjou, which he would inherit in 1481, already belonged to the cadet branch of the Valois. Work was carried out from 1465–67 by Jean Bourré, captain of Langeais, loyal servant of Louis XI and builder of the château of Plessis-Bourré.

LEFT-HAND PAGE:
Louis XI's château.

ABOVE:
Remains of Foulques Nerra's keep.

Marriage of Charles VIII and Anne de Bretagne at Langeais Castle, 6th December 1491

"For this solemn event, despite her straitened circumstances, Anne de Bretagne displayed great opulence in her retinue and clothing ...

... What surpassed everything was the wedding gown, made of gold cloth embroidered with raised patterns picked out in gold relief, thus giving rise to the term 'raised-line gold cloth' for this material. An ell of it was worth 7,350 francs. Eight ells were used for the duchess's robe. (...) At first, the robe was lined with fine black Lombard lambskins, but it was decided this lining was not rich enough and it was replaced with sable, for which 160 skins were used (...) Moreover, Anne de Bretagne had given robes of silk velvet to the gentlemen, ladies and maids of honor, and also to the officers of the household who accompanied her."

Vie de la Reine Anne de Bretagne
Le Roux de Lincy (1806–69)

ABOVE:
Roof of Louis XI building.

LEFT-HAND PAGE:
The access staircase at the entrance is a 19th-century invention constructed after the moats were filled in.

LAVARDIN

The keep.

Henri de Bourbon, Duke of Vendôme, the future King Henri IV, to discourage local and religious squabbles. In 1590, it had been recaptured from Leaguers who had made a last stand there.

The Duke of Vendôme's castle mentioned in the early 11th century must have been built of earth and timber, and was located where the ruins of the keep are. All the buildings of which traces remain are the work of the squires of the local Lavardin dynasty, to whose custody the House of Vendôme had entrusted the site. The castle is of the "barred spur" type, occupying a rocky salient controlling the valley. It is cut off from the rest of the plateau by a powerful keep, the centerpiece of the defensive system occupying the highest point. The core of this rectangular keep was constructed around 1070. The round towers at the corners and the chemise (the low enceinte surrounds it) were added later. The internal layout was entirely remodeled around 1380–84.

Ruin has voided this great chimera of its entrails and exposed its skeleton. At the foot of the keep lies a natural platform on which the residential buildings stood; lower down there was a second platform taken up by outbuildings. These two platforms were protected by the 12th century enclosure wall rebuilt in the 14th century. Substantial parts of the houses, outbuildings and walls are still standing today.

The medieval fortress of Lavardin was a stronghold of the counts, subsequently dukes, of Vendôme. It was pulled down during the Wars of Religion by its legitimate owner

THIS PAGE:
*The central area with the
principal rooms.*

RIGHT-HAND PAGE:
*Small rooms in the turrets built
in the 14th century.*

LOCHES

The fortified enclosure is over a mile in circumference, and was constructed in the 12th and 13th centuries. It embraces a spur which controls the Indre Valley and is cut off from the plateau by a huge moat. On the south side of the spur is the keep; on the north the royal quarters; in the middle, the collegiate church of Notre Dame, built in the mid-12th century. The whole site constitutes one of the most complete groups of buildings to survive from the Middle Ages. A fortress at Loches is mentioned in the 6th century. Rebuilt several times, it passed to the powerful Count of Anjou, Foulques Nerra, the Black Falcon, who probably began building the imposing 120-foot high keep around 1030. It is among the best preserved keeps in France. The entrance is 10 feet from the ground, with access via a secondary tower alongside. In the late 12th century, possession of Loches was disputed between Richard the Lionheart, his brother John and Philippe Auguste. In 1249, Louis IX bought the castle, which remained a crown possession. Charles VII and Louis XI were happy to live in the royal quarters built in the late 14th century. Charles received his favorite Agnès Sorel there, and her tomb gave its name to the Belle Agnès tower. Under Charles VIII and Louis XII, the royal residence was doubled in size, in the Flamboyant Gothic style. The collegiate church of Notre Dame (now Saint Ours church) is remarkable for its sculptured doorway and unusual pyramidal vaulting.

Agnès Sorel and Charles VIII

Perceiving that the King, Charles VII, was enamored of her and cared for nothing except making love to her and, spineless and indolent, paid no heed to his kingdom, (Agnès Sorel) said to him one day that, when she was still a girl, an astrologer had predicted to her that she would be loved and attended by one of the most valiant and courageous kings of Christendom; and that, when the king had done her the honor of loving her, she thought that this was the valorous king who had been predicted; but, seeing him so spineless, with so little care for his affairs, she realized that she had been mistaken and that this courageous king was not him but the king of England, who fought so beautifully and took so many fine towns from under his nose. "So," she said to the king, "I am going to find him, because he was the one the astrologer meant." These words pricked the heart of the king so strongly that he began to weep; and from that time forth, taking courage and abandoning his hunting and his gardens, he took the bit between his teeth; such that, by dint of his honor and valor, he chased the English from his kingdom.

Pierre de Brantôme, *Vie des dames, illustres* 16th century

The keep. On the left-hand page the keep proper can be discerned, onto which the little keep was built. The latter is almost as tall as its big brother. Both date from the 12th century. Built onto the little keep are late 15th-century or early 16th-century constructions.

The keep at Loches

From the end of the 15th century right up to the Revolution, the keep at Loches was used as a prison. One might say that it was saved by its prisoners. It was there that King Louis XI shut up his victims in iron cages. These were no legendary instruments of torture — thanks to the royal accounts, we know exactly how much they cost. The contemporary chronicler Philippe de Commynes, who spent eight months in one, describes them in his *Memoirs*: "harsh prisons covered with iron claws inside and out, with terrible iron fittings the height of a man plus one extra foot." A drawing in the Gaignières Collection reproduces one of these cages.

LEFT-HAND PAGE:
The oratory of Anne de Bretagne in the royal house. Anne married Charles VIII and then Louis XII. The decoration features the ermines of the arms of the dukes of Brittany and the cord of St. Francis, which Franciscan monks wear as a belt and which Anne de Bretagne used as a personal emblem.

ABOVE:
Doorway of the church of Saint-Ours (the ancient collegiate church of Notre Dame). The doorway without a tympanon may derive from the poiton style of Romanesque. The sculpture is divided into three registers: the upper register shows the Adoration of the Magi, the middle two scenes which are difficult to identify (Annunciation? Visitation?), the lower St. Peter and an unidentified episcopal saint.

LE LUDE

On the left, the Louis XII façade. The view inside the walls shows the entrance to the courtyard, at the end of which is the main house. On the right is a close-up of a tower, showing Louis XII's porcupine emblem.

A castle is first mentioned at Le Lude in the 10th century. It was rebuilt several times in the Middle Ages and in 1457 it was bought by the de Daillon family. It was probably Jean II de Daillon, chamberlain to Louis XI and governor of the province of Dauphiné (†1480), who started work on the present château, but the bulk of the work was done by his son Jacques II, chamberlain to Louis XII and François I (†1532). This square, moated château, with its round towers, originally had four wings enclosing a court-yard. The courtyard façades were rebuilt in the second half of the 16th century. In 1785, the architect Jean-Benoît-Vincent Barré rebuilt the entrance and rear wings. The

whole château was heavily restored in the mid-19th century.

The exterior façade of the left wing possibly goes back to the works carried out for Jean II de Daillon by the master of works Jean Gendrot, but the equestrian statue of Jacques II is a 19th-century invention. The exterior façade of the right wing is one of the most remarkable works of the Renaissance style in the Loire area. It can be firmly dated to 1520–30, is the work of Jacques II and almost entirely untouched by restoration. The order is initiated from the François I wing at Blois, and the towers from Chambord. Much is made of the terrace at its foot, which stretches between the two towers, and is bordered by

the moat; it is said to be an innovation. But the bas-reliefs on the balustrade, which represent porcupines, the emblems of Louis XII, are not where they originally stood. Once again, restoration has obscured historical evidence. The façade of the Louis XVI wing, often criticized for having destroyed the unity of the ensemble, has at least the merit of presenting itself for what it is, and is in any case the work of one of the great architects of

Rear façade of the main house.

THIS PAGE:
*The 19th-century
staircase.*

OPPOSITE:
*The gallery with a
fireplace bearing the
Daillon arms.*

the time. The interior conceals a remarkable little room, painted in a scheme representing the triumph of Chastity, various subjects borrowed from the Old Testament (notably the story of Joseph in the pit) and grotesques rather like those executed at Fontainebleau. The decoration was carried out between 1559 and 1585 for Guy de Daillon and Jacqueline de La Fayette, his wife. The models were taken from illuminated manuscripts belonging to the family, notably a manuscript of Petrarch's *Triumphs* painted around 1515. The room is sometimes described as an oratory; it is in fact a *studiolo* in the Italian tradition, and one of the few preserved in France.

THIS PAGE:
*19th-century decoration
framing late 16th-century/
early 17th-century paintings
depicting guards which gave
this vestibule its name.*

RIGHT-HAND PAGE:
The 19th-century staircase.

Closet decorated with paintings that were probably commissioned by Guy de Daillon (†1585) or his wife Jacqueline de La Fayette. Their subject matter is derived from various sources, notably an illuminated manuscript of Petrarch's Trionfi *painted for Jacques de Daillon, the builder of the château. The theme of the complicated iconography is the fidelity of wives and loyalty to the king.*

LEFT-HAND PAGE:
The Triumph of Chastity.

THIS PAGE:
The scenes in the lunettes show the story of Joseph, the son of Jacob and Rachel and faithful servant of the Pharaoh. Bottom left is the meeting of Jacob and Rachel at the well. On the right, the despair of a wife on learning of the death of her husband.

LUYNES

THIS PAGE:
View of the bailey, showing the entrance to the courtyard, at the back of which is the house.

RIGHT-HAND PAGE:
Rear façade of the main house.

The original castle belonged to the Maillé family and bore its name. A reconstruction was undertaken in the 13th century, of which a high rectangular curtain wall remains, flanked by round towers. A large part of the space thus enclosed was taken up by the keep, which was demolished in the 17th century.

The Maillé castle played an important part in the Hundred Years' War, as is evident from the title "English keep", bestowed on the main building, probably after a war-time reconstruction. The long residential building dates half from the late 15th century and half from the late 16th or early 17th century.

The first half was built for Hardouin de Maillé IX. It was a typical small house in the brick and stone style of the period, with a spiral staircase, thick rib vaults and tall dormers. Unfortunately it suffered a heavy-handed restoration in 1875-80.

The second half was built for either Guy de Laval or Charles d'Albert. The Lavals owned Maillé throughout the 16th century, but in 1619, Charles d'Albert bought the title of Comte de Maillé, and in the same year was

raised to the peerage as the Duke of Luynes, the family seat of the Alberts in Provence.

Charles d'Albert figures in both the footnotes and the mainstream of history. As a page, he won the favor of Louis XIII by training his hawks. He took part in the conspiracy to rid the king of the tiresome Concini. Indeed, he accumulated honors to such a degree that he became virtual master of the kingdom. He died in 1621 just before disgrace caught up with him. He thus had only four years to carry out his modernization of Luynes.

MEHUN-SUR-YÈVRE

All that remains of this castle, famous for the reconstruction carried out by Guy de Dammartin between 1367 and 1390, are touching ruins.

Dammartin was architect to Duke Jean de Berry, the king's brother. The original castle was a massive fort that may have dated back to the 12th century. The architect cut into the entrance wall and built onto it a chapel in open work as delicate as fretted gold. He let numerous tall windows into the other fronts and, finally, he topped the towers with lavishly decorated open belvederes.

An illumination in the famous 15th-century *Très riches heures du duc de Berry* (The Duke of Berry's Book of Hours) shows this virtuoso creation, one of the first examples of the Flamboyant style that spread through the realm under Charles V. One of its principal promoters was Jean de Berry, patron of the arts, collector, and builder. For the first time, the art of defense played second fiddle to the art of living. Until the early Renaissance, Mehun remained a paradigm for the châteaux of the Loire Valley.

Only ruins are left of the castle built by Jean de Berry. The castle figures in the illuminated book of hours (the Très Riches Heures) commissioned by Jean, on a page depicting the Temptation of Christ in the Wilderness. Musée Condé Chantilly.

Meillant

Meillant is a château in the Bourbonnais well to the south of Bourges. Running past it is a little tributary of the Cher whose waters flow into the Loire.

Meillant did not join the Ligerian family until the 15th century, with the arrival of the Amboises. At the time, there was a century-old castle whose buildings followed the outline of a polygonal wall completely enclosing the courtyard (the latter was opened out only in the 18th century). One of these buildings was rebuilt by Charles I d'Amboise (d. 1481), another by his son Charles II (before 1510). With its relative simplicity, the former is typical of the architecture of the reign of Louis XI – Charles I

LEFT-HAND PAGE:
Left, the stair tower known as the Lion Tower (after the lion at the top of it). It was built for Charles II d'Amboise before 1510 in a Flamboyant Gothic style which scarcely differs from that of the dormer (left) belonging to the building constructed between 1473 and 1481 for Charles I d'Amboise. The Lion Tower shows no trace

of Charles II's experiences in Italy. The decoration features the monogram of Charles and the 'burning mount' (chaud mont) of the Amboise Chaumont family.
Right, crown of the doorway of the Lion Tower. The dual interlaced Cs are again visible, referring to Charles II and the emblem of the 'chaud mont'.

ABOVE:
Rear façade of the château. The middle part dates from the 14th century. The block with two dormers (left) was built between 1473 and 1481 for Charles I d'Amboise.
The block with one dormer and the square tower (right) are 19th-century additions.
In the background is the chapel.

LEFT-HAND PAGE:
End section of the 14th-century house. At the back, the chapel.

ABOVE:
The small loggia above the fireplace in the drawing room is an odd 19th-century invention. It is adorned with paintings relating to the history of the château.

was chamberlain to Louis. The second, with its stair tower in the Flamboyant style, is one of the most remarkable examples of the style, which was at its height during the first expeditions to Italy but which borrowed only its taste for ornament from Italy.

As Charles II had been the king's representative in Milan, the memorialist Brantôme had good reason to say that "Milan made Meillant."

Nevertheless, there is no trace of Italianism in the superb tower covered in interlaced Cs and burning mountains ('chauds monts'), the emblems of Charles II, who also owned the château of Chaumont in the Loire Valley. But there is record of a gallery decorated with medallions of Roman emperors; these had been placed in the château and originally certainly came from Italy.

ABOVE:
Room remodeled in the 19th century in the Meillant style.

LEFT-HAND PAGE:
Joseph, the son of Jacob, explaining his dream to his brothers. Bruges tapestry, 16th century.

The chapel, with 16th-century altar, altarpiece and stained glass window.

MENARS

Front view. The wings and main house date from the 17th century. The terrace between the wings was added by Soufflot after 1764.

The château developed around a mid-17th century building comprising of a long, low block between two pavilions constructed for Guillaume Charron, councillor to the king and General Treasurer Extraordinary of War. His son Jean-Jacques commissioned the French-style gardens and the two splendid avenues planted with elms which give a superb view of the Loire and its environs.

The two most famous owners were Louis XV's favorite the Marquise de Pompadour and her brother the Marquis de Marigny, the King's Director of Buildings. Between them, they managed to remodel the 17th-century building almost completely.

Madame de Pompadour acquired Menars in 1760, and commissioned the king's architect Jacques-Ange Gabriel to expand and

*Rotunda (Rotonde de
l'Abondance), built by Soufflot
in front of the orangery.*

redecorate it. Marigny inherited it from his sister in 1764, and called in Gabriel's rival Jacques-Germain Soufflot.

Frequent changes of ownership in the 20th century have vastly altered this masterpiece of 18th-century art. Nevertheless, some fine traces of the interior decoration designed by Gabriel remain. The vases and statues decorating the gardens were sold and replaced by copies. Soufflot's garden follies have been reduced to two: the rotunda dedicated to Abundance, which provides a link between the château and the orangery, and the nymphæum in the large lake. The nymphæum is filled with souvenirs of Italy both ancient and modern, which Marigny picked up during his tour there with Soufflot in 1749–51. The columns imitate the squat Doric style of the Greek temples at Paestum, discovered by Soufflot.

*Rear view. The central part dates
from the mid-17th century. The two
wings on the same alignment were
added by architect Jacques-Ange
Gabriel.*

Features of the decoration created for the Marquise de Pompadour and her brother the Marquis de Marigny by Gabriel and Soufflot. The decoration forms a transition between the rococo style and a more austere manner heralding the Louis XVI style.

The Marquise de Pompadour, the Marquis de Marigny and the return to the grand manner

For the uninformed, Pompadour means rococo. It was, however, when the Marquise's hold over the King's affections had begun to fade that there first appeared 'a return to the grand manner', that of Louis XIV. The Petit Trianon, already so "Louis XVI", was in fact constructed for la pompadour during Louis XV's reign by the royal architect Jacques-Ange Gabriel, though she died before she could take possession. It was she who had her brother appointed Director of Buildings. To learn the job, the future Marquis de Marigny traveled around Italy for two years, guided by Soufflot, whose art was to illustrate the Marigny doctrine: neither rococo frivolity nor the severity of antiquity, but the French style.

On the subject of the Chinese temple which Marigny wanted to build at Menars, Soufflot wrote to him: "A Director General under whose administration good architecture has reappeared in France after an almost total absence of 30 years, should build for himself neither in the Chinese nor in the Arabesque manner." To which Marigny wittily replied: "I agree with you as to what a leader of the arts ought to do; but you will agree that it is my person and not my position that resides at Menars."

MONTGEOFFROY

Louis-Georges-Érasme, Marquis de Contades and Marshal of France, built Montgeoffroy between 1772–76. He followed the layout of an older château and reused parts of it, reproducing a type of French château that had been developed a century earlier. There is no trace here of the innovations of the parisian avant-garde, which proved so influential for the decade. Yet, the inclusion of this château in an anthology of châteaux of the Loire is perfectly justifiable, given the relative rarity of châteaux of this period in a region whose main architectural achievements date from the preceding centuries. And Montgeoffroy is preserved in its 1770 condition, down to its original furniture and furnishings, which is extremely rare. The Revolution spared it, just as it spared the Marshal, who did not emigrate; he enjoyed the protection of his grandson Hérault de Séchelles, a member of the National Convention and son of a by-blow. Moreover, the preservation of the château archives provides a remarkable example of the way the construction of a provincial château was handled at the end of the Ancien Régime. The project was drawn up and decided on in Paris between the Marshal, whose duties allowed him to go to Montgeoffroy only occasionally, and the Parisian architect Jean-Benoît-Vincent Barré. Barré carried out other work in the area, at Le Lude, but his most ambitious and original work is the beautiful neo-classical

PRECEDING PAGE:

The entrance front. To frame the 18th-century house, the two towers of an early period were intentionally preserved, bearing witness to the antiquity of the place. The exceptional interest of Montgeoffroy lies in its furnishings. Made by Parisian cabinet makers and tapestry weavers, they were designed at the same time as the architecture and interior decoration, and have remained just as they were.

château of Le Marais near Paris. It is perhaps surprising that the same architect should have produced such different works, but the laws of the genre explain this: old nobility and a provincial château on the one hand, and the Île-de-France and new money on the other.

In all probability, Barré did not even bother to visit the site. The architect in charge, Simier (Gilles or Pierre?), was a local. Judging by their correspondence, his relationship with his Parisian boss must have been strained. He knew the site well, but his justifiable criticisms were regarded by the Marshal as little short of insubordination. Montgeoffroy has the perfection of tried and tested models, this may owe more to Simier than we imagine.

MONTREUIL-BELLAY

Most of the building work on this château overlooking the River Thouet was carried out for Guillaume d'Harcourt and Yolande de Laval, whom Guillaume married in 1454. The couple died in the early 1480s.

Their work, one of the most typical examples of the Renaissance style of the second half of the 15th century, and thus still Gothic in style, did not completely obliterate the layout of the medieval castle; indeed, it seems to have been reused very extensively. The enclosure wall with its thirteen towers was rebuilt on the old foundations. Either the fabric of the old buildings was used or medieval attitudes still prevailed, for the new buildings are scattered around the courtyard in complete disorder. The keep, probably the one built by Foulques Nerra, Count of Anjou, in the early 11th century, stood in the middle of the courtyard until the 19th century, proudly proclaiming the antiquity of the family who owned it.

The Château Neuf (New Château) with its great spiral stairtower, a sign of the greatest distinction at that time, and the collegiate church, served by a chapter of canons can safely be attributed to Guillaume d'Harcourt. (It was by the number of prebendary canons in their collegiate church that great lords measured their power, just as the landed gentry measured theirs by the number of pigeonholes in their dovecotes.) Putting an accurate date on the entrance barbican, the Château Vieux (Old Castle) adjoining it, the kitchen, and the canons' quarters is more complicated. The ensemble is partly or wholly the work of Guillaume's builders. This type of kitchen with a central hearth, covered with a pyramidal vaulted roof with an opening at the top to let out the smoke, was quite common at one time but there are very few surviving examples. In chronological terms, the kitchen at Montreuil-Bellay lies midway between the monastic examples, generally from the 12th century, and the model illustrated in Philibert De l'Orme's treatise of 1567. It too seems likely to have been built by Guillaume.

The odd feature of Montreuil-Bellay is the canons' accommodation, comprising four

PRECEDING PAGE:
The gatehouse with its two towers. On the right is the Château Vieux.

ABOVE:
The Canons' House. It consists of four small similar dwellings, each having its own separate stair tower.

RIGHT-HAND PAGE:
The drawing room.

little manor houses each with its own stair tower. They are more reminiscent of Carthusian monasteries or *béquinages* than canonical quarters; we are particularly reminded of the château of Ripaille with its row of seven pavilions, created in 1434 for the knights of the Order of St Maurice. Inside the canons' quarters are bath-houses, another oddity; they bear the Harcourt arms and were presumably built by Guillaume. The house must be several decades older. The Harcourt family had owned the site since 1415, and Guillaume inherited it in 1428.

The chapel of the Château Neuf, decorated with paintings from the second half of the 15th century.

MONTSOREAU

View from the courtyard side. The buildings which enclosed it were demolished.

No château had a greater claim to be 'of the Loire' than Montsoreau, whose walls are bathed by the Loire a mere five cables' length from its confluence with the Vienne, though a 19th century road now lies between château and river. All that is left is a large main house flanked on the river side by two heavy square towers and extended to the rear by two truncated wings. Once, the courtyard was closed and the towers bore pavilion roofs. This was the château built in 1455 for Jean de Chambes, a member of Charles VII's privy

The Lady of Monsoreau

This was the title of a novel by Alexandre Dumas, which made the château famous without its 't'. In it, Dumas describes the intrigues at the Valois court at the end of the 16th century, in which the Duke of Anjou attempts to seize the crown from his brother, Henri III. These doings form a background to the romance between Bussy d'Amboise and the fair Diane de Méridor, married against her will to the lord of Monsoreau. The historical Diane in fact married Charles de Chambes, great-grandson of the builder of the château. The following extract describes the first meeting of the two lovers.

"Suddenly, the woman in the portrait stepped out of the frame, and there advanced towards him an adorable creature, clothed in a long gown of white wool like those worn by angels, with blond hair falling about her shoulders, eyes black as jet, long velvety eyelids and a skin beneath which it seemed one could see the lapping of the blood which imparted her rosy complexion. This woman was so prodigiously lovely and her outstretched arms were so alluring that Bussy made a violent effort to go and throw himself at her feet. (...)

At the sight of this woman, the characters depicted on the walls and the ceiling ceased to engage Bussy's attention. Everything else had ceased to exist for him."

Alexandre Dumas
La Dame de Monsoreau

ABOVE:
Upper parts of the staircase. Note the slates which fill the gaps in the parapet.

council sent by the king on numerous diplomatic missions to Italy. The date of 1455 is provided by a royal decree authorizing tax-free transport of the lead and wood required for the construction. The château still has the appearance of a fortress, but it is only an appearance; the machicolation is strictly ornamental. The return of security after a hundred years of war made it quite unnecessary to strengthen château defenses. The main house is served by two stair towers with spiral staircases at the angles of the courtyard. They are both undoubtedly original. But the bay comprising the entrance to the right-hand tower has been entirely

rebuilt in the Italianate style of the early Renaissance. This sort of treatment of bays with superposed pilasters first appeared at Gaillon in 1510. The parapet crowning this tower is formed of a tracery in which the lights are simulated in slate. Round slate mouldings of this kind are a feature of royal châteaux built during the ligerian Renaissance.

MORTIER-CROLLES

Mortier-Crolles is not one of those fortresses of menacing aspect in which the Loire Valley is so rich. It is a baronial country house, enclosed less to thwart external attack than to protect private life while clearly manifesting its baronial status. In the second half of the 15th century, there seems to have been a vogue for these houses. Réné de Provence proved an illustrious exponent of the fashion in his Duchy of Anjou; but there is no more significant example than Mortier-Crolles.

The high wall marks off an almost rectangular quadrilateral defended only by angle towers. It is pierced not by loopholes but by windows which here and there look out onto the fields. Possibly these provided light for timber buildings that once backed onto the enclosing walls but have now disappeared. The enclosed area was originally divided into three parts: the bailey to the left (north) was entered via the barbican; on the right is the garden; and finally, contiguous with these, is

The chapel, seen from the passage through the barbican.

the central courtyard with the house and chapel.

Construction of the castle as a whole has been attributed to Pierre de Rohan, the famous Maréchal de Gié, who won fame under Louis XI, Charles VIII and Louis XII, and took part in the Italian wars. At Verger, in the Loire Valley, de Rohan built a château famous for its magnificence and modernity.

The Flamboyant decoration here, in which the occasional Renaissance motif is found,

undoubtedly dates from the period when the powerful Marshal (†1513) was lord of Mortier-Crolles. But the mascle, the heraldic lozenge of the Rohan blazonry which crops up here and there, is not a reliable chronological indicator since Mortier-Crolles belonged to the Marshal's family well before he took possession of it. A clearer chronological indicator is the radical transformation that makes the château so picturesque today. The lower part of the

enclosure wall with its towers and the solid mass of the barbican and main house are built in local shale rubblestone – this is the Breton aspect of the house. None of this proves the house to be the work of the Maréchal de Gié. By contrast the entrance façade of the barbican, with its two towers, the two right-hand angle towers, the upper section of certain parts of the curtain wall and the chapel are built in a curious bond alternating of brick and stone layers. The brick is of local manufacture, but the stone is a calcareous tufa brought from the Loire by river and offloaded on the banks of the nearby River Oudon. The use of a decorative bond marrying brick and stone is at least one indication that Mortier-Crolles pertains to the Ligerian châteaux. Who, if not from the courtier who served three kings, could have clothed the old Breton château in the latest fashion? Did modernization suddenly stop for lack of money or was the Marshal content with buildings that bore witness to the antiquity of the house? The integration of a garden within the wall, if it dates from the 16th century, is also an innovation. Moreover, the two angle towers of the enclosure wall have the status of independent manors or guesthouses in which to lodge vassals or friends.

The chapel. The masonry is made up of beds of brick and stone, designed to be seen from the outside, where it shows to remarkable effect. The interior must have been plastered, perhaps as a preparation for frescoes.

Overall view of the château.
On the left is the main house.

Le Moulin

The rebuilding undertaken around 1480 by Philippe Du Moulin, who obtained permission to fortify his castle in 1490, was unfinished in the early 16th century. It shows no trace of Philippe's participation in the first royal expedition to Italy. The random distribution of buildings on a platform surrounded by moats is Gothic, but the peculiar effect that the arrangement produces today, when the buildings appear to have been placed on the site like pieces on a chessboard, is due to the partial disappearance of the surrounding wall. The tall, narrow main house with its stair tower central to the facade, a matching stair tower at the rear, and a chapel at the side, is typical both of small contemporary châteaux, and indeed of Gothic manor houses. Le Moulin is one of the most notable examples of the marriage of stone and brick, exhibiting the geometric tracery of glazed bricks so fashionable in late 15th-century Loire houses.

Nantes

Duke François II of Brittany and his daughter Anne (Duchess of Brittany and, thanks to her marriages to Charles VIII and Louis XII, Queen of France) built this château. Escutcheons party per pale of France and Brittany, the hedgehog of Louis XII, and Anne's ermine, their mottoes, and the letter A abound in the decorated areas. This is partly accounted for by the enthusiasm of the restorers, but we must give some credit in the matter of construction to Anne, who lived on for another twenty six years after succeeding her father in 1488. François II, Duke of Brittany from 1458, chose Nantes for his principal seat, and in 1466 commissioned Mathelin Rodier, master of works at the cathedral, to undertake the reconstruction of the castle. Little is left of the first castle built in the 13th and 14th centuries at the southwest corner of the town walls. And the buildings added after the death of Anne are of little importance, in quality if not in volume. The

stylistic unity of the late 15th-century château, at once fortress and palace, is striking. The fortified outer walls, flanked by towers, have survived in their entirety, with the exception of the northern corner which was destroyed in an explosion in 1800.

The towers were designed to accommodate artillery. The horseshoe tower, so named for its ground plan, was an artillery tower of the very latest design. Its location on the east wall is no accident: war with France was imminent. This 'war of independence' came

to an end with Anne's marriage to Charles VIII. From the 1480s, most of the forts in the Duchy were put on a defensive footing and equipped with such horseshoe-shaped artillery towers.

Yet in many respects the château of Nantes formed part of the civilization developing in the Loire Valley. François himself had been brought up at the court of Charles VII and until the beginning of the 19th century the waters of the Loire lapped at the south front of Nantes. The palace is made up of two large buildings that meet at the Tour de la Couronne d'Or (Golden Crown Tower). The narrower building, which is probably the older, was called the Ducal Palace until the name was changed in the 17th century to Government House. At the same time, a flight of steps was built mid-façade, probably to replace a spiral stair tower. The explosion in 1800 destroyed the northern half of the staircase, which led to a chapel.

The second building, wider and more ornate, is called the Grand Logis (Great House). This was due to be completed by a wing, of which the toothing stones can still be seen. No doubt this would have been even more splendid, with southern prospects and views over the Loire. It is quite possible that Anne built the Great House in its entirety, though only the upper parts are normally ascribed to her.

The Golden Crown Tower, so called after the (now vanished) corona on the well at its base, contains nothing but two staircases. These interconnect only at top and bottom. The small spiral stair is on the ducal palace side and a larger spiral stair on the Great House side. The disposition of grand and private staircase was common in châteaux of the time, but only here are they combined in a single tower.

Can we therefore conclude that the Ducal Palace, served by the small staircase, was reserved for the private apartments, and that the Great House was reserved for reception rooms? The façade of the Ducal Palace has the south-easterly aspect recommended for residential buildings. The Great House is divided in half by two transverse interior walls, set close to each other and constituting an obstacle to the creation of large reception rooms. One is no doubt the vestigial gable wall of an older building. The parallel wall was no doubt intended to replace it and this create a suite consisting of one large and one small room. The most unusual part of the whole château is the upper part of the Golden Crown Tower, which is formed of a pair of loggias. The lower one connects the two staircases, while the upper one extends the belvedere crowning the Grand Staircase.

These loggias, probably commissioned by Anne de Bretagne, are drawn from the Loire repertory. Their existence alone would be enough to justify the inclusion of a Breton château in a book dedicated to the châteaux of the Loire. The ambiguity of the Ligerian château of Brittany, as in numerous other châteaux, becomes clear in the use of materials – shale and Breton granite for the fortress, Ligerian limestone for the house.

Golden Crown Tower. It contains two staircases which interconnect only at top and bottom. The larger one, on the left, serves the Great House (the reception rooms), while the smaller one on the right serves the Government House, the ancient ducal residence. The connection at the top is effected via two open loggias.

OIRON

Front view.

The left wing of the château was built in the 16th century by Artus and Claude Gouffier and the main house and right wing in the 17th century by Louis Gouffier and the Duke de La Feuillade. The right wing was completed after 1700 by Madame de Montespan.

Nothing remains of the castle rebuilt by Guillaume I Gouffier. His son Artus, who took part in the first Italian expeditions, had the good fortune to be appointed tutor to the Count of Angoulême, the future François I.

When François became king in 1515, Artus was appointed Grand Master of France, or governor of the king's house. Before his death in 1519, he had time to build the lower gallery of the left wing and the collegiate church alongside the château; the church was completed by his widow, Hélène de Hangest. In the *collégiale* are buried Guillaime's wife, Artus, Guillaume II (Artus's brother, the famous admiral of Bonnivet, who commissioned the huge château of Bonnivet in

BELOW:
View of the right wing. The left wing and its round tower (perhaps a reuse of a 15th-century building) date from the 16th century, though the dormers were replaced in the 17th century. The main house and its huge pavilion blocks were commenced in 1620 for Louis Gouffier and completed in 1670–80 for the Duke de La Feuillade. The right wing with its round tower (possibly also a 15th-century survival) was built for the Duke de La Feuillade and finished for Louis XIV's mistress Madame de Montespan, who bought Oiron in 1700.

THIS PAGE:
Painted decoration at the foot of the great staircase, 16th century.

RIGHT-HAND PAGE:
The great gallery of the left wing, one of largest in France. Decorated for Claude Gouffier with scenes from the history of Troy. The painter was Noël Jallier, mid-16th century.

Ceiling of the great gallery. The ceiling is original, but the naive decoration was added in the 17th century.

Poitou, now destroyed) and finally Claude, Artus's son. The tombs are attributed to a distinguished family of sculptors, the Justes.

Claude's career was as brilliant as that of his father, but lasted somewhat longer. He was appointed Master of the Horse in 1546, and lived until 1570. He built the remarkable staircases with straight flights and half turns. On its lower part, his monogram is found alongside that of Jacqueline de La Trémoille, his first wife, whom he married in 1526. On its upper part, his monogram accompanies that of Françoise de Bretagne, whom he married in 1545. In the middle, it bears the date 1544. In the lower gallery, built by his father, the Master of the Horse, no doubt a reminiscence of the famous gallery at the Palazzo del Tè in Mantua there are "portraits" of horses, on the upper floor of the same wing, Artus built a gallery which he decorated in 1545–49 with fourteen scenes depicting the Trojan War or extracts from the *Aeneid*. With the exception of the François I gallery at Fontainebleau, they are the finest and most extensive set of 16th-century murals in France. The artist was possibly the Frenchman Noël Jallier; but the composition owes much to the Fontainebleau painters Rosso and Primaticcio.

THIS PAGE:
*Above, ninth scene of the Trojan War,
showing the death of Hector.
Below, eleventh scene of the Trojan War,
depicting the flight of Aeneas.*

RIGHT-HAND PAGE:
*Eighth scene of the Trojan War, showing
the combat of Paris and Menelaus.*

The subservient lords of Oiron

The lord of Oiron was technically a vassal of the lord of Thouars. Such was the subjection of the Oiron estate to that of Thouars that, at any time the lord of Thouars so desired, he could instruct his neighbor at Oiron that he would be hunting on such and such a day in his neighborhood and that he must demolish a certain number of lengths of wall in his park so as to leave no obstacle should the hunt chance to enter that way. One can see that this is such a harsh right that no-one would think of exercizing it. But equally one realizes that there are occasions when it will be taken full advantage of; and then what will become of the lord of Oiron?"

Saint-Simon, *Mémoires*, 1691–1701

ABOVE:
*Tenth scene of the Trojan War,
showing the Trojan horse.*

RIGHT-HAND PAGE:
*Straight-flight staircase, with
half-turn, built for Claude
Gouffier, 1535–40.*

PRECEDING PAGES:
Muses Room, decorated with the figures of the nine Muses, executed around 1630–40 for Louis Gouffier.

ABOVE:
Great Chamber on the first floor of the main house. Decorated ceiling 1630–40.

Collegiate church, built by the
Gouffiers to accommodate their
tombs and dedicated in 1532.
The doorways and oratory
(r.h. page) were added between
1535 and 1540 for Claude
Gouffier. The tomb is that of
Philippe de Montmorency,
grandfather of Claude
Gouffier, and was erected by
the latter in 1539.

Le Plessis-Bourré

Le Plessis-Bourré is considered a prime example of the early French Renaissance of the second half of the 15th century. This was an economic, demographic and political renaissance that owed nothing to Italy. One aspect of it was the careers of the new men in the service of the king. Jean Bourré, who bought the domain of Plessis in 1462, was a member of the country bourgeoisie. Ennobled in 1465, he made his fortune in the service of Louis XI. The châteaux of the reign were made in the image of this pragmatic and thrifty king. At Plessis-Bourré, as at Langeais, the château built for Louis XI under Bourré 's

supervision, defense work was discreet and ornamentation sparse. These creations are more modern in spirit than those built by later and more prodigal kings, flush from the Italian wars and infatuated with chivalry.

Le Plessis-Bourré is preceded by a fore court reconstructed in the 17th century, and surrounded by wide moats. The four wings form an almost square courtyard with four round corner towers. In this traditional layout, the sole innovation is the lowering of the entrance and lateral wings, and the consequent domination of the rear wing, thus clearly identifiable as the main house. Light,

ABOVE:
The courtyard, showing the entrance opening into it. The arrangement of the open galleries is in the medieval tradition.

LEFT-HAND PAGE:
View from the entrance side. The bridge links the chateau with the service buildings. The bridge and entrance define a central axis, in a rough attempt to regularize the ground plan.

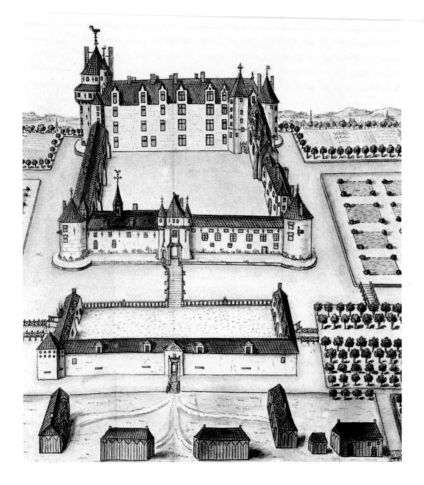

ABOVE:
View from the entrance side.
Drawing from the Gaignières
Collection (1695).

RIGHT-HAND PAGE:
Rear view.

The great hall of the house.

The gallery. This occupies the whole length and breadth of the left wing facing the courtyard. It is heated by two fireplaces, like the gallery at the town house of Jacques Cœur in Bourges. The gallery, covered a kind of promenade whose exact use is not clear, is one of the basic components of the French house.

air and views were in this way bestowed on it, along with the logic imported by a central axis running from forecourt to main house. With peace promised and in the main delivered, high curtain walls could be lowered, but the château was not disarmed. It is equipped with an all but invisible *dans-œuvre* rampart walk with machicolations at the entrance tower and the bulkiest of the round towers. This tower is fortified like a keep, but you have to be inside it to perceive the fact. Decoration on the façades is minimal. Bourré himself is credited, perhaps wrongly, with the whole construction, though evidence of reuse is abundant. The work was certainly finished by the early 1470s – not without difficulty, because

Basement. Remains of a skylight.

Jean Bourré and Louis XI

Jean Bourré had been appointed by Louis XI to high offices which normally kept him away from the building work that he had initiated, in his desire to have a château worthy of his rank. Bourré was unable to leave Amboise, where he had the care of the Dauphin, whose health was precarious. His requests to the king for permission to go to Plessis and inspect the work in progress were often refused.

A letter from Bourré, who was at Amboise:
"Sire, Monseigneur the Dauphin is thanks be to God and Our Lady in a very good way, and since it does not please you to give me leave to go on a journey to my house, may it please you at least to send word to me that it will be your pleasure that I may go for eight days only ... because I have much work to do there of necessity..."
The king's reply:
"Monsieur du Plessis, I have seen what you wrote to me. You shall *not* go to your house."
A letter from the king recalling Bourré, who was at Le Plessis:
"Monsieur du Plessis, straightway at the sight of these letters hasten in my direction with all diligence as I have occasion to speak with you. I have always been agreeable to your excusing hitherto, but for the matter I have for you now I cannot excuse you and I pray you, putting aside all excuses, set forth in my direction forthwith."

The Guards' Room, with a painted narrative ceiling from the early 16th century.

Bourré was constantly being detained by the king who refused to allow him to go and supervise the works. "You will *not* go to your house," replied Louis XI to a written request.

The remarkable painted ceiling, which has been dated to the early 16th century, may have been commissioned by Bourré, who died in 1506. But its ornamental function and Italianate structure contrast strongly with the rest of the château. A full interpretation has yet to be made; several of the subjects are enigmatic. A reading of some scenes suggests that the scheme as a whole is an illustration of proverbs. One shows a she-wolf with every rib showing. This is Chicheface, whose

stomach is so delicate that she can thrive only on a diet of virtuous women. She is consequently starving.

In its general approach, the château of Plessis-Bourré heralded a type of château that might be called "civil", in both meanings of the word. But the absence of exterior signs of success was only a phase, and a very short one, in the style of King Louis XI. Fortification and ornament soon became a feature of all great houses, and especially those of the parvenus, a class to which Jean Bourré belonged.

ABOVE:
Ceiling of the Guards' Room.

*Six of the 24 scenes and figures that grace the ceiling of the Guards' Room. The interpretation of the scenes remains uncertain.
Left to right and top to bottom: siren with mirror; anguipède and spinner;* fountain; singing donkey; two dogs; *the* chicheface *of legend.
The* chicheface, *identified by an inscription as the she-wolf that eats only virtuous women, is depicted as starving.*

LE PLESSIS-MACÉ

In the 11th century, there was a timber-built castle at Plessis-Macé; in the twelfth century, a stone castle contributing to the forward defense of Anjou. The lords of Le Plessis-Macé took part in the Angevin expedition to the Kingdom of Sicily. In 1427, after a century of neglect, the castle was bought by the de Beaumont family. In the second half of the 15th century, Louis de Beaumont and his son Thibaut rebuilt it entirely. There is little sign of the fact. Within its fortified enceinte, buildings are scattered around as they must have

been in the 12th century. The keep, standing by itself in the bailey, was rebuilt on its *motte*.

Louis de Beaumont was chamberlain to the Duke of Anjou, and later, when Anjou reverted to the royal demesne under Louis XI, to the King of France. Louis XI lavished favor on him, dubbing him one of the first knights of the Order of St. Michael. This explains the dedication of the chapel, which contains

an extraordinary openwork gallery with Flamboyant tracery in wood.

Le Plessis-Macé is near Le Plessis-Bourré, built by another of Louis XI's favorites. In keeping with the spirit of the times, the work of the parvenu financier Jean Bourré is highly innovative; that of the soldier, the noble Louis de Beaumont, is not. The former seeks to attract attention, while the latter no longer needs to.

La Possonière

Courtyard facade of main house.

La Possonière has conserved the basic layout of a 14th and 15th-century manor: a bailey and courtyard intercommunicating via a passageway flanking the manor house; the house is served by a stair tower with a spiral staircase that forms the prime feature on the courtyard side; aligned with the house and the passageway are two barns completing the separation of courtyard and bailey; the outbuildings cut into the hillside as right angles to the courtyard.

The transformation carried out in the 1510s by Loys Ronsard, though he confined himself to moving partitions and rebuilding bays and chimneys, is wholly engaging. Loys Ronsard served the Duke of Orléans, who made him a gentleman of the royal household. As a consequence, he took part in all the Italian wars. He retained his position under François I, who appointed him majordomo to the Dauphin. When the king, captured by the Emperor Charles V, was exchanged for his two sons, Ronsard shared the Dauphin's captivity in Spain.

The highly original decoration of the bays and chimneys is, when all is said and done, only a mixture of Gothic and Italian motifs, a formula that characterizes the entire decorative repertory of the early French Renaissance. But the effect produced at La Possonière is unique. No doubt this is due both to unusually precise quotations from Italian art and their transformation by a treatment that was evidently local. Loys Ronsard must have drawn on his recollections of Italy; but it has been shown that the artist also followed models in engravings.

The decoration at La Possonière is touching; it is full of symbols, emblems and heraldic figures and exhibits innumerable inscriptions. With some exceptions (the fleur-de-lis, François I's salamander, and the Ronsards' burning rose-bush – ronce ardente) the

emblems remain enigmatic. The inscriptions are pagan and Christian mottoes and maxims. The "sustine et abstine" is a Latin translation of Epictetus' motto; Ronsard may have found it in the *Adagia* of Erasmus

Door of stair tower.

LEFT-HAND PAGE:
Door with inscription 'Tibi soli gloria' (Thine alone be the glory), from St. Paul's Epistle to the Romans. This door, which led to an unidentified building, may have belonged to a chapel.

THIS PAGE:
The outbuildings. They are in part hollowed out of the rock.

published in 1513. It means "endure and forgo", or more generally "forgo the pleasures that may do harm to the soul." The maxim reappears several times, notably on the door of the kitchen! The "voluptati et gratiis" may have been lifted from the *Liber de Voluptate* written by the Platonist Marsilio Ficino in 1497. This is, by contrast, an invitation to enjoy life, though *voluptas* is not only the pleasure of the senses but also of the mind and the soul. In all, 18 Latin and French inscriptions made up the mural 'commonplace book' of the young Pierre Ronsard. The poet, Loys' son, was born at La Possonière in 1524, and there discovered the rudiments of his humanist culture.

THIS PAGE:
Above: kitchen window in the service buildings, with the inscription 'sustine et abstine' (endure and abstain).
Below: a room in the service quarters cut into the rock.

RIGHT HAND PAGE:
Fireplace in the great hall. It is covered with the emblems and monograms of the Ronsard family and ornaments directly borrowed from Italian models popularized by engravings.

Les Réaux

ABOVE:
Front view. On the extreme right, the towers of the entrance pavilion. Leading on from that, the 18th-century wing.

RIGHT-HAND PAGE:
The keep (left) and entrance pavilion.

Of the 16th century château, which was once called Plessis-Rideau or Plessis-Macé, there remains the entrance block flanked by two round towers and the keep. The salamander of François I and ermine of Queen Claude are still visible on it, and it must have been constructed for Jean Briçonnet, who inherited it at the beginning of the reign. The château is one of the most remarkable examples of the decorative style obtained by a mixture of brick and stone masonry. It received its present name in 1653 by means of letters patent issued at the demand of Gédéon Tallemant des Réaux, the famous author of the *Historiettes*, who had acquired the château in 1651. In the 18th century the entrance pavilion was flanked by a wing longer and higher than the seemingly 16th-century wing opposite, which was actually built in 1897.

SAINT-OUEN

An old chapel, a new house and an older house on the same alignment go to make up the château of Saint-Ouen. The outbuildings, which completed the ensemble until the 19th century, have since been lost. The first building is perhaps the chapel mentioned at the end of the 12th century; it was then under the jurisdiction of the Abbey of La Roë. In the 15th century it underwent a transformation, and today it is no longer used for worship. The old house is a classic example of the 15th-century manor house: a long main building, flanked in the middle by a stair tower with a spiral staircase containing the entrance. This modest residence, sadly lacking in ornament, is probably from the early 15th century.

The new house is merely an enlargement of the old one; again, a long house, a stair tower, and dormers with high gables. But the project as a whole is on a much larger scale and is decorated in a style half Flamboyant, half Renaissance. This house is also flanked at the rear by two blocks which may have been added later, in the late 16th or even early 17th century, despite the Gothic ornament. The 17th century was quite capable of imitating earlier decoration in order to guarantee unity of style.

Building a second house was a commonplace phenomenon in domestic architecture, but few have survived to exhibit such a powerful contrast between old and new. Like many other rural buildings, the whole group is built in locally quarried shale rubblestone with a covering of plaster. Only the façade and stairtower use ashlar masonry of Saumur limestone.

The construction of the new house is attributed to Guy Leclerc de Coulaine, who was elected Abbot of La Roë in 1493 but took office only in 1495. In his later career he was chaplain and counsellor to the queen, Anne de Bretagne, until 1506 at the latest, then to her daughter Claude de France, and finally became Bishop of Saint Pol-de-Léon in 1514.

ABOVE:
Staircase of the New House.

OPPOSITE:
Main fireplace of the New House.

The château belonged to the abbey and it was in his capacity as Abbot that Leclerc had the usufruct. The new house is not a homogeneous construction. We can distinguish several phases of construction, even before the addition of the pavilions at the rear. They are: the construction of the main house, its subsequent extension, and the construction and subsequent upward extension of the stair tower.

The main phase can be dated to the period 1505–23, and was certainly commissioned by Guy Leclerc, whose GL monogram and heraldic eaglets figure prominently in the interior decoration and on the stair tower. In 1505, he persuaded the Abbey to cede title to the château; he died in 1523. The staircase may be contemporary with the Louis XII staircase at Blois, with which it has features in common; this dates it to 1515 or before. It was (or should have been) at the centre of a symmetrical façade, accessing two rooms per floor, each lit by a single window in the façade. This symmetry was destroyed when the main house was extended by adding a bay to connect with the old chapel. The upper floor of this additional space contains the only vaulted room. Though identified as Guy Leclerc's room, it was probably an oratory or closet, communicating with the ground-level room below via a secret staircase. This lower room had no openings for light or passage and was used as a strong room. Numerous legends are associated with it. The stair tower terminates in a room which has been called – no-one knows why – the queen's bathroom, and has a roof terrace. The arguments put forward for dating this extension to the same period as the lower part are not convincing. We need only mention the theory based on the presence at the top of a frieze of wheels, emblems of the Abbey of La Roë. After the death of Guy Leclerc, the abbots of La Roë continued to live at Saint-Ouen, or at least to alter its fabric, as they did with the top of the tower in the early 17th century.

SARZAY

In the foreground, the only surviving tower from the curtain wall. Three of the original four towers of the keep can be seen. The stairtower lacks machicolation and is probably a later addition.

Sarzay is among the southernmost châteaux included in this volume. Close to a tributary of the Indre, it stands in the foothills of the Massif Central. The type of castle formed by a square or rectangular keep with round angle towers, protected by a curtain wall incorporating further towers, originated in the royal demesne at Vincennes, near Paris, after 1450. The keep of Sully-sur-Loire, built by the architect royal very late in the 15th century, stands as an intermediary between Paris and

Sarzay, which was probably built in the first half of the 15th century for the Barbançois, a family deeply involved in the Hundred Years War. Sarzay numbered 38 towers in its curtain wall. Only one remains, converted to a chapel. The fifth round tower of the keep is the stair tower, and is unusual in this kind of château. Access was generally through an angle stairtower, or wooden staircases rising through the floors. Sarzay's stairtower is probably a 17th century addition.

Side of the keep. The
machicolation dates it to the
15th century. It is the largest
surviving part of a fortress with
extensive curtain wall and
towers.

Saumur

Early in the 13th century, Philippe Auguste reclaimed Anjou from the king of England. As a result, during the minority of Louis IX, fortresses were constructed beside the Loire at Angers and Saumur, the latter dates from around 1230. In 1360, Charles V created the duchy of Anjou for his brother Louis. The buildings of Charles V and his brothers, the dukes of Berry and Anjou, were fundamental to the evolution of the seignorial residence. The two main innovations were the use of monumental spiral staircases for distribution and ostentation, and the borrowing of open-work techniques from religious architecture. The spiral staircase built at Saumur in 1371 rises from the ground right up to the roof.

Amply lit from the front and decorated with niches whose sculptures were intended to glorify the Valois dynasty, the staircase is our only remaining evidence for the direct influence of the great newel staircase of the Louvre. Saumur is one of the few châteaux to appear in the illuminations of the *Très Riches Heures* of the Duke of Berry. Yet it was not an innovative building. It seems unlikely that the Duke of Berry lent his brother the inspired architect of Mehun-sur-Yèvre, Guy de Dammartin; the name of the Duke of Anjou's master of works, Macé Darne, is known from the records. The latter was content to rebuild a closed castle on the foundations of the 13th-century fortress, with four wings (one of them destroyed in the 18th century) flanked by four corner towers. Yet it was his idea to build polygonal towers with angle buttresses on the round stumps of the fortress towers, thus foreshadowing the pilasters of the towers at Chambord. He scattered fleurs-de-lis and weathervanes on the crenelation and roofing, gratifying the taste of contemporary Valois princes for florid rooflines. None of this has survived. But he did not dare to follow Dammartin in using great tracts of openwork, which would have weakened the defenses. These were strengthened in 1590, at the end of the Wars of Religion, by the construction of bastions designed by an Italian engineer known to us only by his first name, Bartolomeo.

RIGHT:
South front, with the entrance.

ABOVE:
*The courtyard. The main house
(left) is positioned between the
Loire and the courtyard.*

RIGHT-HAND PAGE:
The oratory on the first floor of the château, where the north and east wings meet, forms part of an ensemble extensively remodeled during the time of King René (15th century). The keystone in the vaulting is decorated with interlaced figure-of-eight patterns (lacs d'amour). The lac d'amour was adopted as an emblem by René in honor of his second wife Jeanne de Laval.

THIS PAGE:
Detail of façade.

SELLES-SUR-CHER

Moat front of the buildings in the outer bailey.

At Selles, we are presented with two châteaux in one. The bailey of the present château is that of the medieval castle. Although the first building probably goes back to the 10th century, there is no trace of it in the fortifications of the bailey, everything being part of the rebuilding commenced in 1212 for Robert de Courtenay. This work

was itself heavily altered by rebuilding in the early 17th century.

Interest focuses on the later building, a handsome house of Renaissance elegance, commissioned by Philippe de Béthune, younger brother of Henri IV's great minister, the Duke of Sully. Béthune's brilliant diplomatic career did not allow him to follow the work closely; it was

completed in 1612. But there is no doubt that he chose one of the great architects of his time, possibly Jacques II Androuet Du Cerceau. The general arrangement is that usually called Henri IV or Louis XIII: a mixture of brick bond and stone, tall main blocks, and an imposing portico in closing in the courtyard wall. The style is a highly sophisticated variant Mannerism.

Systematic destruction was begun in 1788. State finances required the destruction of many a royal château at the same time as a change in taste exposed private châteaux to the same fate. The Revolution cannot therefore be blamed for this campaign of vandalism, which was fortunately not comprehensive.

In the foreground, the moat front of one of the pavilions of the main quadrangle.

"Among all these visits, a frequent visitor was the Countess of Béthune, whom I had gone to see at Selles, which is a very fine and very pleasant house beside the River Cher. The apartments there are fine, comfortable and well-furnished. She and her husband received me there perfectly well and even the old fellow, the late Monsieur de Béthune, did everything he could to express his pleasure to me. The presence of this distinguished person gave the house a particular air; his worth and the reputation that he had acquired in the important tasks he had undertaken, principally on two missions when he had been to Rome, made him a figure of special respect for everyone. He was all the more revered for the regard that my grandfather the king had shown him in appointing him governor to my late uncle, the Duke of Orléans [who died at the age of four]. The ability and heroic virtues that conferred the honorific the Great on King Henri IV and made him an inimitable example to those that are to come, were such that this distinction in itself was capable of creating a favorable opinion of a man."

A second visit in 1653:

"I went from there to Selles, which is a fine house and one that I have already spoken of. The Count of Béthune and his wife did the honors of their house very well, with a hospitality as magnificent as that at Valençay. I found much of interest at Selles. The Comte de Béthune has a great number of very fine pictures. As I am no judge of painting, it was not the finest of these that engaged my attention. The portraits of famous men of Europe and particularly those of the king's court, my grand-father, the late king, my uncle and another of the latter with some placards saying what they had done of note in their lives principally attracted my attention. He has manuscripts to look at, in fact there are an infinite number of volumes. I took great pleasure in reading the letters of the king, my grandfather, and all the accounts of that period. I should never have been bored in that place where I spent one day ..."

Mémoires of Mademoiselle de Montpensier, known as the Grande Demoiselle, posthumous edition, 1838

The two pavilions and enclosing side of the main quadrangle.

SERRANT

View of the rear façade.

The recent discovery of a contractor's agreement dated 14 November 1539 has raised a question mark over the date at which construction is thought to have started, around 1550. In this as yet unedited contract, made available to us by its discoverer, Dominique Letellier, a researcher at the Inventaire Général, the carpenter André Cousin contracts Félix de Brye, representing his brother Péan de Brye, lord of Serrant, to roof a house with two corner towers and with a central block containing the staircase. The master mason Jean de Lespine, who witnessed the deed, was very active as a

master of works in Angers and may have been the architect of the main house, which was then being built. In 1636, the *seigneurie* was bought by Guillaume de Bautru. During the 17th century, the wings were completed, maintaining the original style. At the end of the right wing is the chapel attributed – on no good evidence – to Jules Hardouin-Mansart. It contains the tomb of the Marquis de Vaubrun, killed at the Battle of Altenheim in 1675. The tomb was commissioned in 1677 by his widow from the painter Charles Le Brun, who provided the design, and from the sculptors Collignon and Coysevox.

View from the entrance, showing the doorway and two small pavilions; the main house and the two wings facing the courtyard; and one of the round corner towers.

The Duchess of Berry at Serrant

The widow of the assassinated Duke of Berry was the daughter-in-law of King Charles X and mother of the heir to the throne, the Duke of Bordeaux. She therefore had every reason to be a fervent legitimist. She was welcomed ecstatically by monarchist Anjou, particularly on 16th June 1828 at Serrant.

"A triumphal arch marked the entrance to the park. As the princess's carriage passed under the arch, a shower of roses, strewn by young boys dressed in the costume of the Béarn region, fell on the royal head. It was magical: the sun was shining brightly; cries of 'Long live the King, long live Madame, long live the Duke of Bordeaux' mingled with the harmonious tones of a military band ... In the distance banners bearing fleurs-de-lis fluttered at the tops of towers. The cannon thundered out in the midst of the rejoicing; a flag was draped over every tree, each bearing a royal device. Everywhere, the rejoicing came from the heart."

Comte Walsh, *Souvenirs*, 19th century

In the great drawing room, a 17th-century Brussels tapestry. The cabinet is also 17th-century, and is by the noted ébèniste Jean Macé.

SULLY-SUR-LOIRE

The most celebrated owner of Sully was the man who acquired the *seigneurie* in 1602, Henri IV's great minister Maximilien de Béthune. The *seigneurie* was upgraded to a duchy in 1606. But the château has greater claims to our interest: its "keep" was built right at the end of the 14th century for Guy de La Trémoïlle, who married the heiress to the castle, Marie de Sully, in 1382.

Guy de la Trémoïlle was the Duke of Burgundy's head chamberlain, and viewed the keep as a work of prestige; he used it exclusively for receptions. Beside the "keep" or "great castle", the site contained a lesser "château" that acted as a residence for the lord, an outer bailey in which stood an early keep erected by Philippe Auguste following a confiscation of the fief, and a collegiate church which Béthune transferred to the town.

A further remarkable feature is the system of canals, still extant, excavated by Béthune to prevent floods. The man responsible was the celebrated Raymond du Temple, the architect royal, who transformed the Louvre for Charles V.

In the foreground, the Great House inappropriately called the keep. In the background (right) is the Little House.

TALCY

The construction of this little château, still in the 15th century fashion, is attributed to Bernard Salviati, a merchant in the service of François I who acquired the *seigneurie* in 1517 from the heir to the Simon family. In 1520, Salviati gained a license to construct a "fortified house", though without being entitled to call himself lord of the manor or have a watch and sentry. At the heart of the kingdom and at the beginning of the century, the fortifications were, in the event, no more than an outward show of nobility. In short, it does not seem that Salviati, scion of an important Florentine family, made use of the license. He seems to have been content to occupy the château in the form that he acquired it in 1517, preferring a style evocative of the ligerian bourgeoise to the expense of unnecessary fortifications. Talcy has its place in literature. The Cassandra of Ronsard's Amours was Bernard Salviati's daughter, and Diane de Talcy was celebrated by Agrippa d'Aubigné.

ABOVE:
The drawing room.

RIGHT-HAND PAGE:
The press.

The 'Amours' of Ronsard and Agrippa d'Aubigné

The first group (of poets) was from the end of the François I's reign and that of Henri II, and we will name Monsieur de Ronsard their leader, whom I knew privately. Our acquaintance grew when my first affections became attached to Diane de Talcy, the niece of Mademoiselle de Pré who was his Cassandra [Cassandra, daughter of Bernard Salviati, who married the lord of Pray, a year after meeting Ronsard]. I urge you, and those who will listen to me, to read and re-read this poet above all. It was he who cut the thread that tied the tongue of France.

Agrippa d'Aubigné, letter to a correspondent

When these fair eyes decree that I must die
And banish me below before my time;
And when the fates have led my steps

Across that utmost stream to banks condign;
Cave field and copse who mourn me then
Have pity on my fate and do not scorn;
But give me 'neath the shadow of your arms
A dwelling-place eternal and forlorn.
And may some amorous poet not yet born
Have pity on my lamentable fate
And on a cypress let him carve its rhyme:
Here lived a veritable lover of Vendome,
A victim of her rigour here he lies,
His crime: to love to well those faust eyes.

Pierre de Ronsard, *Les Amours de Cassandre*

USSÉ

Entrance wing.

Construction of this magnificent château was the work of the Bueils, one of the most important families in the area, and the Espinays, who first bought Ussé in 1485. It is believed that work was begun by Jean V de Bueil († 1477) but the bulk of the work was carried out by his son Antoine, who married King Charles VII's illegitimate daughter Jeanne de Valois. Ussé was sold to Jacques d'Espinay, chamberlain to Louis XI and later to Charles VIII († 1523). He and his son Charles († 1535) completed the château.

The château was originally built with an enclosed courtyard. The wing overhanging the River Indre was demolished in the 17th century to open up the courtyard to the river. The keep and the collegiate church stood outside the courtyard. The church was constructed in the 1520s for Charles d'Espinay and his wife Lucrèce de Pons, whose initials C and L are prominently represented. Quite a number of large Loire Valley châteaux founded in the second half of the 15th century or early 16th century have

collegiate churches, that is, chapels distinct from private castle chapels, isolated from them and served by a chapter of canons maintained by the lord.

The portal of the collegiate church of Ussé, consisting of a doorway and a large window enclosed in the same frame, is very

characteristic of the period and the genre; Flamboyant Gothic ornamentation mingles with Italianizing Renaissance motifs. The latter are rare in the château itself.

The Bernin de Valentinay family, who bought Ussé in 1659, opened up the courtyard and built, on the same alignment as the

Interior of the courtyard. Entrance wing (left).

*View from the Indre.
In the middle, the courtyard,
opened up to the river in the
17th century. On the right is the
new house built at the same
time. Behind it is the keep.*

demolished wing, a new house with a view over the river. As Louis II de Valentinay had married the daughter of Vauban, the famous military engineer, the latter has been credited with supervising the 17th-century works. In fact, this role was probably performed by the Abbot of Saint-Hilarion, the owner's cousin, to whom the great staircase can safely be attributed.

Major additions and restoration were carried out by the Countess of La Rochejacquelein, owner of Ussé from 1829 to 1883.

VALENÇAY

The entrance pavilion.

RIGHT-HAND PAGE:
The gallery adjoining the entrance pavilion.

All that is left of the original château, which had four wings round a rectangular courtyard, is the entrance wing and main house. The heavy round tower that marks the corner where the two meet was probably built around 1520–30 for Louis d'Estampes, governor and bailiff of Blois. It is reminiscent of the contemporary towers at Chambord, but it was subsequently covered by a dome. This must have been the first building on the site.

The heavy building that marks the center of the wing and incorporates the entrance bears the date 1599. It was built for Jean d'Estampes, who married a rich heiress, Sara d'Happlaincourt, in 1578. A monumental building, it is a curious testimony to the persistence of the Loire style of the beginning of the century.

The main house gives further proof of the care taken by the owners to preserve unity of style. Half of it is from the same period as the corner tower; the remaining half was built in the mid-17th century for Dominique d'Estampes, first Marquis de Valençay.

The same applies to the large round tower which completes the main house and forms a pair with the older tower. It was built in 1767 for the Farmer General Legendre de Villemorien who instructed his architect Joseph Abel Couture to complete the external facade in 16th-century style, but to finish the courtyard in a "modern" style typical of the last years of the reign of Louis XV, a style now known as Louis XVI. In 1803, the château was acquired by Talleyrand.

**Napoleon imposes on Talleyrand, the owner of Valençay,
the custody of the dethroned Spanish Bourbons**

"The Prince of Asturias, the infante Don Antonio, his uncle, the infante Don Carlos, his brother ... will be at Valençay on Wednesday. Be there on Monday evening ... I desire that these princes should be received without ostentation, but civilly and with interest, and that you should do everything possible to amuse them. You could take Madame de Talleyrand there with four or five ladies. If the Prince of Asturias should become par-ticular with some pretty woman, it would be no calamity, especially if one were sure of it ...

As for your part, your mission is altogether honorable: to receive three distinguished personages in your home in order to amuse them is wholly in the character of the nation and in that of your position."

Letter from Napoleon to Talleyrand (9 May 1808)

VERDELLES

In January 1491, Hardouin de Maillé instituted proceedings against his vassal Colas Leclerc for having "undertaken construction in the form of a castle and fortress in the place called Verdelles: which he neither can nor ought to do because he is not a lord castellan." The suzerain demanded the demolition of the "castle and fortress." The judgment handed down in 1494 was favorable to Colas Leclerc, who had produced letters from Hardouin de Maillé "by which he had allowed the said squire to make the said edifices as would seem good to him." The château derives, wholly or in part, from these late 15th-century works. The "castle and fortress" is made up of a square central house flanked by four towers. The two angle towers on the left are themselves square and crowned with machicolation. The angle towers on the right are polygonal. The front one contains the main doorway, leading on to the great spiral staircase. The courtyards, forecourts and moats usual in a late-medieval château have not survived. Interpretation of the surviving elements is problematic. The house with its four towers is clearly not homogeneous, although it is often presented as such. The central house and the towers on the left bear witness to a desire for symmetry, which, had it succeeded, would have produced a château with four towers at right angles to the square central house. The regularity was perhaps greater than it appears. Time has partially obliterated a certain unnevenness of the terrain; if this were restored, we should see that the two square towers, today unequal, were of equal height. Such square towers with machicolation and pavilion roofs are typical of the second half of the 15th century (those at L'Isle-Savary, are similar); in fact, they are all but identical to the tall pavilions of the 16th and 17th centuries.

It is hard to date the two polygonal towers. The stair tower is the splendid fruit of Flamboyant work which cannot be later than the early 16th century and which extended throughout the château (doors, windows, fireplaces) with the exception of the polygonal tower at the rear. The polygonal staircase tower would be regular were it not for the large slope that is tantamount to a hipped roof. It had to merge with the curtain of the enclosure wall so well that the irregularity was not noticeable, "intra muros". The rear tower, tall, solid and almost blind, has a more or less regularly pentagonal ground plan; this is architecture for troubled times, and may date from the time of the Wars of Religion.

The château of Verdelles, which, until the Revolution, belonged to the descendants of Colas, the powerful Leclerc de Juigné family, is linked to the Loire châteaux by the neighboring River Vègre, a tributary of the Sarthe.

VILLANDRY

In 1533, Jean Breton (or Le Breton) acquired the little château of Colombiers, which he then rebuilt almost entirely and called Villandry, after one of his *seigneuries*. Breton was General of Finance for the county of Blois, and had just been appointed Comptroller of Wars. His château of Villesavin en Blésois no longer matched his prosperity, and his fortune was such that he could have started from scratch. In the event, he preserved a tower from the château of Colombiers at the angle of the main house and the right wing; the latter was obviously built on ancient foundations whose irregularities it follows. It was standard practice in pre-Revolutionary architecture to reuse foundations to save money, although this was covered up wherever possible. On the other hand, the preservation of old towers, which spoiled the symmetry of ground plans, was used again and again to proclaim the antiquity of sites.

From 1526, the court normally resided in the Île-de-France. Villandry is a late-season château exemplifying the Ligerian fashions of the 1510s and 1520s; Île-de-France influences are also perceptible. The latter are said to explain the two blocks at the end of the wings which have no antecedent in the Loire Valley. But we must be careful when interpreting these two blocks, since they must have been altered when the wall closing the courtyard was demolished.

The removal of the wall, which was

In the background, the château. External façade of the Renaissance wing facing the courtyard on the right. The angle towers survive from an older castle.

ABOVE:
The courtyard. In the corner on the right are remains of an older castle.

RIGHT-HAND PAGE:
Gardens recreated in the 19th century on 16th-century models.

intended to open the outlook from the main house, is typical of the alterations undergone by Renaissance châteaux in the 17th and 18th centuries. It was probably the work of Comte Michel-Ange de Castellane, who acquired Villandry in 1754 and carried out major rebuilding. Dr. Carvallo, who bought the château in 1906, partly obliterated this work while claiming to restore the building to its original state. However, this practice, as we now know, only makes us doubt the authen-

ticity of what we see. Fortunately the great 18th-century staircase was spared – rather than replaced by a '16th-century' replica. Carvallo's major work was the restoration of the gardens, which made (and make) the reputation of Villandry. Gardens existed as early as the 16th century and these were reconstructed following the evidence of engravings, especially those in *Les plus excellents bastiments de France*, (1576–79) by Jacques Androuet Du Cerceau.

VILLEGONGIS

The main house with its two solid round towers was built in the early 1530s (inscribed dates of 1536 and 1538 mark the completion of the decoration) for Jacques de Brizay, *lieutenant général* of Burgundy, and Avoye of Chabannes, a Bourbon on her mother's side.

The plan called for galleried wings on both sides of the court, which may or may not have been built in the 16th century. If they were erected in the 17th century, following a different arrangement, only traces remain today.

The *dans-œuvre* (integrated) dogleg staircase, the upper parts of which are missing, belongs to the school of Renaissance-style châteaux, while the decoration and sheer size of the towers link the château of Villegongis with that of Chambord.

These features connect Villegongis, which stands on the fringes of the Massif Central, with the Ligerian châteaux.

VILLESAVIN

ABOVE:
The external façade is distinct
from the courtyard front.

RIGHT-HAND PAGE:
Detail of the same façade.

This château is thought to have been built entirely between 1527 and 1537 for Jean Breton (or Le Breton), a financier whose brilliant career as culminated in the post of Comptroller General of Wars under François I. The ornamentation certainly belongs to the 1527–37 period, but the general arrangement could be fifty or a hundred years younger. The symmetry of the main quadrangle, extended to the right by the outbuildings and to the left by the farm, the ground-floor *piano nobile* covered only by the roofspace, a small block flanking the main quadrangle – all this is very surprising for the time. True, the

D'UNE GRANDE FORET UN PETIT BOIS VC AN
ICI VIT AUTREFOIS NAITRE VILLESAV,
QUI BIEN QU'AYANT SUBI DES ANS LE LONG OUTRA
ORNE ENCOR BEUVRON LE CHAMPETRE RIVAGE

BATI EN 1557 PAR N. LEBRETON SIEUR DE VILLANDRY
SECRETAIRE DES FINANCES DU ROI FRANCOIS 1er

LAIS DES VALOIS

DANS UN B

château of Villandry, also built by Jean Breton, includes the innovation of angle pavilions, but these are on a quite different scale.

Its modern aspects may have come into being in the early 1540s, when the first French works by Serlio appeared. Serlio's publications and drawings were the more influential in France for the fact that he sought to reconcile the regularity of Italian ground plans with the convenience of French ones.

The avant-corps that marks the center of the façade on the quadrangle side of the main house is a 19th-century addition.

ABOVE:
Overall view of the courtyard.

LEFT-HAND PAGE:
Centrally placed avant-corps of the main house on the court side.

THIS PAGE:
The Flagellation.

RIGHT-HAND PAGE:
Chapel, richly furnished with early 17th-century paintings, linked to the second school of Fontainebleau.

Glossary

Arcade
A series of arches freestanding or blind.

Ashlar
Dressed stone with even faces and edges laid in horizontal courses.

Avant-corps
Part of a building projecting from the main block, like a porch.

Barbican
A castle-style or building within a castle, especially a gatehouse.

Barred spur
Loire Valley castles were often built on a promontory which could be isolated by digging a defensive moat across the spur where it joined the plateau. The moat 'barred' the promontory or spur against attackers.

Bay
The unit or block of structure from one support to the next, e.g. from one pillar to the next in a church.

Bond
The pattern of bricks or masonry laid to give strength to a wall, e.g. lengthways, overlapping, etc.

Château
A seignorial or royal mansion/country house built mainly for residential purposes, especially in the Renaissance period.

Collegiate church
A medieval church attached to a château and staffed with salaried canons.

Curtain wall
The outer defensive walls of a castle.

Dans-œuvre
Used particularly of staircases, it defines constructions fully integrated into the orthogonal ground plan. Earlier staircases were contained in towers contiguous with the façade.

Dogleg staircase
A staircase with straight flights and no stairwell; the stairs turn 180 degrees at the landing.

Dormer
A window set in a roof with its own roof and sides.

Escutcheon
The shield shape on which a coat-of-arms is drawn.

Fief
The estate held by a feudal lord. Fiefs could be divided into fractions, such as quarter-fiefs, held by different people.

Gallery
This can be a series of arches making a covered walk, like an 'arcade', or the open first-floor level in a medieval church, or a very long room in a château.

Gatehouse
A collective term used to describe any large fortified building over the entrance of a castle.

Gothic style
A medieval building style, characterized by pointed arches and rib-vaulting. In fashion until the end of the 15th century in France.

Ground plan
A diagram showing the outline of a building on the ground and the arrangement of the rooms.

Hall
The principal room of a castle or house in the Middle Ages.

Illuminated
Illustrated with hand-painted, colored scenes and figures and usually made in a monastic scriptorium.

Keep/donjon
The powerful central defensive building of a medieval castle. In early days, both lord and retainers lived in it.

Ligerian
The adjective from 'Loire'. In this book, used to describe buildings in the Loire-valley style.

Loggia
A room open to the air.

Machicolation
Openings at floor level beneath a parapet on a castle, to allow defenders to shoot at or pour things onto attackers climbing the walls.

Marquetry
Inlaid wood patterns in furniture.

Openwork
Open ornamental tracery in Gothic buildings.

Oratory
A small private chapel for the lord or lady.

Outer bailey
The outer courtyard or space inside the outer walls.

Party per pale
Divided by a vertical line through the middle.

Pavilion
In a château, a prominent rectangular block, linked by one or more narrower, lower buildings. A 'pavilion roof' has four equal sides.

Piano nobile
The floor of a house containing the main reception rooms.

Portico
A large roofed, open porch with classical columns.

Return wing
A building at 90 degrees to the main building.

Rubblestone
Walling stone not cut to shape nor set in courses.

Rustication
Masonary cut in large blocks with emphatic, deep joints. The surface of the stone may be ornamentally carved.

Seigneur
The owner of a fief, like a lord of the manor.

Bibliography

WORKS IN FRENCH:

Androuet du Cerceau, Jacques:
Les plus excellents bastiments de France, 1576–79.
New edition issued in 1988 by Sand et Conti, Paris. With an introduction and notes by David Thomson.

Babelon, Jean-Pierre:
Châteaux de France au siècle de la Renaissance. Paris 1989.

Gebelin, François:
Les châteaux de la Loire. Paris 1957.

Guide du Patrimoine en région Centre. Paris 1992, under the direction of Jean-Marie Pérouse de Montclos.

Guillaume, Jean:
La galerie du Grand Ecuyer. L'histoire de Troie au château d'Oiron. Chauray 1996.

Jeanson, Denis:
La Maison Seigneuriale du Val de Loire. Garnier 1981.

Melot, Michel:
Châteaux en pays de Loire. Architecture et pouvoir. Paris 1988.

Pérouse de Montclos, Jean-Marie:
Histoire de l'architecture française. De la Renaissance à la Révolution. Paris 1989.

Toulier, Bernard:
Châteaux en Sologne. Paris 1992.

WORKS IN ENGLISH:

Binney, Marcus:
Châteaux of the Loire. Viking 1982.

Blunt, Anthony:
Art and Architecture in France: 1500–1700. Penguin 1981.

Bony, Jean:
French Gothic Architecture of the 12th and 13th Centuries. University of California 1983.

Swaan, Wim:
Art and Architecture of the Late Middle Ages. Omega 1982.

WORKS IN GERMAN:

Albrecht, Uwe:
Von der Burg zum Schloss. Die französische Schlossbaukunst des Spätmittelalters. Worms 1986.

Prinz, Wolfram and Kecks, Ronald G:
Das französische Schloss der Renaissance. Berlin 1985.